Answering B Questions in Amazon Interviews, Second Edition

Advice for Candidates at All Levels

JENNIFER SCUPI

Visit interviewgenie.com for more information on interviewing at Amazon.

Table of Contents

Note on New Edition

This new edition adds information about the two new leadership principles that were added in July 2021. In addition to that, I've included more sample answers for the questions. I've also added more detailed tips on how to target your answers by job level and more questions that are directly targeted toward managers.

Introduction

Are you nervous about answering Amazon behavioral interview questions?

If you're worried about the behavioral questions at your Amazon job interview, you're not alone.

No one likes behavioral interview questions. Technical people aren't used to talking about their skills in story format, while salespeople don't like sticking to a specific format. New interviewers can't remember all the rules to follow in the answers, and experienced interviewers don't like using such a strict format.

Also, if you're like most people, you've probably forgotten what you did at your old jobs, so the idea of writing stories for the answers seems impossible.

Not to mention it's intimidating to interview with Amazon, the company everyone wants to work for these days, right?

Use This Book As a Guide for Your Amazon Behavioral Interview Prep

If you're worried about your behavioral interview questions, you need a guide on your interview journey who can take you step by step through the knowledge and techniques needed to answer this type of question. This book can be your guide.

There's a lot of information out there about Amazon behavioral questions. But you don't have to read it all yourself. I've put all the necessary information together in one place to make it easy for you to learn what you need.

If you've seen my website – interviewgenie.com – you might have read some of the information I'm going to mention in the book. Through the years, my interview coaching clients have asked me for a guide that packaged up all my posts into a single book. The book and blog are not quite the same – the book includes more examples and additional explanation.

Why Should You Trust Me?

When I started interview coaching, I didn't know much about Amazon. But eventually, after having worked with hundreds of Amazon job seekers, I became an expert on Amazon interviews.

From working with so many candidates, I gained knowledge about how Amazon hires and what it values. I realized the Amazon interview is seen as difficult because of the behavioral questions and leadership principles. The interviewers use these questions because they want to learn about candidates, and they think this type of question will prevent bias in hiring. In helping my clients prepare for behavioral questions, I've learned just how stressful many people find this interview style.

My goal is to share my knowledge with you, the interviewee, so you'll have as little stress as possible during your preparation. I intend to demystify the Amazon interview process and provide a structure in which you can succeed.

After being an interview coach for eight years, there is no one on this planet who has coached more Amazon candidates than I have. I've coached thousands. That is not an exaggeration. I used to say I'd coached hundreds, but I finally had to admit it had gotten into the thousands. I do this full time, and many of my clients these days are Amazon candidates. I also work with candidates applying for jobs at other tech companies as well as non-tech companies, but the largest number of my clients are applying to Amazon.

If you want to know more about me you can look at my LinkedIn profile.

My Information Is Real

The information in this book is based on feedback from successful (and unsuccessful) candidates. The questions I give you to study were all asked during my clients' interviews. The sample answers got the candidates the jobs.

Who Is This Information For?

The information in this book applies to all positions at Amazon, from entry to C level, and all divisions, including AWS. I've had clients interviewing for many roles in different locations like Luxembourg, Germany, the UK, India, and the US, and they all found my information to be useful.

What About the Technical Content of Answers?

I'm not a technical person, so I'm not going to be able to advise you on the technical content of your answers. Behavioral interviewing is a combination of soft skills and hard skills – the ability to communicate and the knowledge of your field. I don't have the knowledge of your field that you have, and in the case of technical job candidates, I won't know much about the technical details. My advice is on the communication or soft skill side of interviewing, although I've seen so many stories I can often tell you if yours fits the pattern I see from other candidates for your role.

Can I Guarantee Results?

I'd like to tell you that every single one of my clients got hired. Unfortunately, many of my clients don't write to me afterward and tell me. Quite a few of them do and that's where I get my information, but not all of them. I understand. We're all busy – who wants to write to their interview coach when they're done with interviewing? That's why I can't give you percentages on how often my services work for my clients.

I can tell you that, if you work with me, your interview skills will be much improved. You'll understand the Amazon interview process, and you'll be prepared to answer their questions.

What will get you the best results is knowledge and practice. I can give you enough knowledge and some practice, but you'll probably have to practice on your own as well if your interview skills aren't great when you come to me and you're on a deadline.

If someone tells you they can guarantee results, they're just trying to get your money. I can help you and I will do my best to make you the best interviewee you can be, but you need to work hard on your own as well.

The Secrets to Successful Behavioral Question Answers

I get a lot of emails from people asking me to send them sample answers they can use for their interviews.

If you read all the chapters in this book, you should know enough to write your own answers using your own successes and failures. I will give you sample answers in each section, which should help you create your own stories. If you go through all the sections of the book and try to create your own answers based on the questions, you'll end up with a portfolio of answers you can use to practice for a successful interview.

I'm not going to write your answers for you because I can't. Even if I wanted to write your stories for you, I wouldn't be able to because I don't know your professional experiences. Only you know that information. If you want to send me the answers you've prepared, I can tell you if they're good and tell you what you need to do to improve them, but I can't write them for you because I don't know your job history.

Is This Book Right for You?

This book can be your guide if you're thinking:

- I don't know what behavioral questions are.

- I don't know what behavioral questions I might get asked in my Amazon interview.

- I don't know what the Amazon leadership principles are, and I don't know how they're used in interviews.

- I don't know how to give answers to interview questions that work well as answers for the Amazon leadership principles.

How to Use This Book

You can start at the beginning and work your way through the chapters in order or just read the ones you need.

After you finish reading, you'll be well equipped to stand out from other applicants and get the offer you want.

For many of you, reading the book and creating your answers yourself will be enough to prepare for your interview. If you've done that and still feel like you want or need more help, I'd be happy to work with you.

We can schedule an interview coaching session or I can read your answers and give you written feedback. My email is jennifer@interviewgenie.com.

Let's get started and get you ready.

Chapter 1. Managing Interview Stress

If you're reading this chapter, you're probably feeling pre-interview stress before your Amazon interview.

Interviews are hard for everyone, but Amazon interviews can be very stressful because Amazon has a reputation for being tougher in interviews than other companies.

Also, Amazon may be your dream company. If this is the case for you, you may be nervous about interviewing there because you're putting extra pressure on yourself to get the job.

To combat stress, you should prepare for the interview. If you feel prepared, your stress will be more manageable. Fortunately, how to prepare is not a mystery.

Let's go over a few things that have helped my clients make it through the Amazon interview process.

Preparation Steps

There are so many articles about how to prepare for an interview, and I don't want to write another one with the same advice. You know you need to get a good night's sleep, eat a good breakfast, etc. You don't need me to tell you those basic things. You came to this book because you want to know about Amazon specifically, so let's focus on tips useful for Amazon interviews.

Practice your answers using the Amazon preferred style

If you know you've got good answers, your stress will be lower. If you don't know what style of answer Amazon likes, keep reading this book.

Don't wait until the last minute to start

You'd be amazed at the number of requests for coaching in which the person tells me the interview is the next day! I realize that sometimes you do get a request for an interview that you can't turn down and it's in a day or two, which doesn't give you much time. However, I also get a lot of clients who had time but didn't use it wisely and now are coming to me at the last minute.

You should start creating your answers as soon as you know about the interview. It's much easier to create your answers over a few weeks than doing it all in one night.

Spend as much time as you can preparing

There is a colleague of mine who prepares clients for the Harvard MBA program interview. He is the best MBA prep coach in the business. He says that he won't work with people until they've already practiced one hundred hours themselves before they come to him. The people who are practicing one hundred hours are your competition – not the exact same people, but the type of person who is willing to do that. If you haven't done enough prep, you may lose the job to someone who has put in that much time.

I love thinking of the MBA coach, because so many of my clients think that one hour of prep will be enough. One hour might be enough if you're already a great interviewer, but not otherwise.

The people who apply to Amazon are the world's overachievers. I understand these people very well because I am the daughter of two, the sister of one, the wife of one, and the friend of many. You can trust me when I say they are preparing every extra second they have before their interview.

Manage Stress During the Onsite Interview

Many interviews have onsite segments. The Amazon interview is no different, in that usually you will have an onsite interview after your preliminary phone interviews.

However, video interviews are increasingly common and during Covid-19 Amazon went to video interviewing.

Whether it's in person or on video, your "onsite" interview day will be long. There are a few things that can help you get through the day.

Be aware – prepare yourself mentally

The onsite interview is not like a normal day at the office. It takes stamina and an ability to deal with stress. You'll have to present your story over and over and be as sharp and focused at 4 PM as you were at 9 AM.

Are you mentally prepared for the experience? Even if it's going to be on video, it can be hard to stay focused all day.

Once you've prepared for the interview questions, you should prepare yourself mentally for the day-long interview so you aren't surprised by how tough it is.

Think about what parts of the day will be hard for you and see if you can plan anything that might help you cope.

Practice with Chime

If your interview is on video, are you comfortable with Chime? If not, you can read the chapter on using Chime.

Breaks

You won't get breaks between every interview. They will often schedule video interviews back-to-back. Sometimes they'll schedule in breaks for you, but not always.

If you need a break, ask your interviewer.

If your onsite hasn't been scheduled yet, ask if you can split it into two days to make it easier (you can tell them you can't be out of the office for a full day).

Have snacks ready

If you need to eat something (during the breaks) to keep your energy up, you should. Keep coffee or water at your desk.

Chapter 2. Amazon Interview Process Basics

You may have heard about the "Amazon interview process." The process isn't exactly the same for each job, but there are some similarities it's useful to understand. The overall process works like this:

1. Screening interviews

    Each candidate should expect at least one but possibly as many as four separate phone screenings. These screenings are 45-90 minutes each and not on the same day.

    If you pass all of these screenings, you will be scheduled for the on-site interview.

    These are called "phone screens" but will often be on Amazon Chime, which is the company's video conferencing platform. Unfortunately, you will know ahead of time whether they want to use Chime but not if they are going to turn the video on, so be prepared for video. I know, that really sucks, right? If it's a phone interview you want to be able to use your notes, but you can't if it's on video – or at least you can't let them see you using notes.

2. Onsite interview / The Loop

    Onsite interviews are also known as "The Loop." The number of people who'll interview you for your onsite depends on the level of job you're applying for, but you should expect to meet with four to eight people. These meetings occur on the same day although you can (and should in my opinion) ask that they be broken up into two days. During Covid-19, the company switched to video interviews on Chime for this phase. See "Video Interviews" for more information on interviewing with Chime.

Screening Interviews

Who conducts the screening interviews?
The process usually starts with a recruiter. After that you will probably talk to the hiring manager or a peer, or sometimes both. The mix, and I say mix because there is sometimes just one call but can be up to four, of people you should expect to talk to is some combination of recruiter or HR manager, hiring manager, and/or future peer.

Are screening interviews difficult?
Don't plan on the screens being any easier than the onsite interviews.

The screening interviewers will ask much the same questions as later interviewers – they won't ask easier questions just because they're conducting a "screening" interview.

The interviewer may focus on going through your professional experience point by point, which they may not do in later rounds, but they will also likely ask you a mix of the other questions as well.

I advise you to take the screens as seriously as the other interviews. After all, if you don't do well with them, you won't go any further in the process.

People ask me this all the time, "But can't I wait to prepare until after I see how the screens go?" Sure, you can, but if you think you need interview prep then why would you wait until after you've already started the interviews? It makes no sense to do it this way. If you need to prep, and you must if you're reading this book, start before the first screening interview.

Loop Interviews

Who conducts the onsite/Loop interviews?

The Loop interviewers will be a mix of positions. Some of them will be in jobs that are related to your position and others will be from different departments. They'll try to have most of them be from jobs related to the position, because these are the people who can best test you, but sometimes people are busy so they can't wait for the perfect line up.

Even if the interviewer won't be your supervisor or colleague, they're still there to test you.

Be prepared for a mix of interviewers. If you're a technical person, you may have to talk to someone who isn't as technical or has different technical skills, so you want to be mentally prepared for this. Be prepared to change your language from technical to non-technical so that they can understand you.

You may know the names of your Loop interviewers beforehand, or the job titles, or only the number of people you'll be meeting.

If they do give you the names, check them out on LinkedIn and review their background. This preparation will help you target your answers. It's okay to look them up on LinkedIn – most candidates do this.

Job Levels

The number of people you'll talk to is the same as the level of job you're applying for. Amazon has a job leveling system that designates the salary and seniority of the job. L stands for "level," with L1 being the lowest and L12 the highest.

I assume if you're applying for a job at Amazon, you're already familiar with the levels, but I'm going to outline it here because it will tell you how many people will be in your loop interviews.

L1–L3 Hourly workers, part-timers, contractors, warehouse workers

L4 Associates/Consultant

L5 Manager

L6 Senior Manager

L7 Senior Manager/Principal/Director

L8 Director/GM

L9 There are none of these

L10 VPs

L11 SVPs

Most of my clients are going for jobs in levels 4-11, although I've worked with candidates for levels 1-3 as well.

If you don't know the level of the job you're applying for, you can use the description above to make a guess. Once you get an actual interview, you can ask the recruiter or hiring manager what the level is.

If you know the level of job, you'll know how many people will be in your loop interviews. If it's an L6, you'll have six people, and so on.

The "Bar Raiser"
"Who (or what) is the 'bar raiser'?"

This is probably the number one question my clients ask me.

The bar raiser is one of the interviewers in the Loop interview.

Are there any clues who the bar raiser is?
The easiest way to identify the bar raiser is to be told and sometimes you will be.

The bar raiser is usually someone who has interview experience at Amazon, meaning they've hired and retained employees, so you can eliminate someone who started a few months ago.

They won't be in the department that is hiring. This is usually the best clue as to their identity.

They'll have probably been at the company at least three years – they're an experienced Amazonian.

What is the bar raiser's task exactly?
The bar raiser decides whether the candidate's answers "meet the bar or raise the bar." In other words, are they average or well above average?

They are not in the department that is hiring, so they are supposed to give a department-outsider, unbiased perspective on the candidate's abilities. Even though the other interviewers are evaluating candidates too, the bar raiser is supposed to have higher standards because they aren't worried about filling the job quickly (since they don't work in the department). The bar raiser is protecting the company from a hiring manager who is so eager to hire someone because they need short-term relief that they might hire an average or below average candidate.

Does the bar raiser have veto power?
Before the hiring meeting, all interviewers write up their notes and vote on the hire. During the hiring meeting, the interviewers share their notes and then discuss the candidate, including their strengths and weaknesses. After this round of discussion, some interviewers may change their vote since they now have more data. A lot of effort is made to reach a decision where everyone agrees.

The bar raiser and the hiring manager will listen to the feedback and then will need to agree for the candidate to get an offer. The bar raiser does ultimately have veto power, but they won't make the decision without input from everyone, most importantly the hiring manager.

Will everyone have a bar raiser in their interview?
Bar raisers are used in interviews mostly for the corporate or professional roles at Amazon, so if you're applying for a job in the warehouse or delivery services, for instance, you don't need to worry about this.

How is the bar raiser going to be different than the other interviewers?

Bar raisers are experienced interviewers who excel at getting data from candidates.

If the interview isn't delivering the right information, the information they need to decide if you're the right candidate, it's their job to fix that. They only have a limited amount of time to get the data they need, so they're under pressure to lead you to answer the question with the information they're looking for.

To get what they want, sometimes they have to be tough and ask hard questions, interrupt if you've gone off track, or ask for another example because the one given didn't yield the right data.

All of your interviewers need to get information from you, but the bar raiser will generally be more experienced at this. Sometimes being questioned by an experienced interviewer can be uncomfortable because they won't ask you the easy questions. They're not trying to make you uncomfortable (most of the time), but you may end up being uncomfortable as a side effect of them trying to get you to answer the question in a way that's useful for them to determine your eligibility for the role.

So how do I prepare for the bar raiser?

Now that you know about the bar raiser, what are my suggestions for preparing for this part of the interview?

In my opinion, it's simple: you prepare for the bar raiser the same way you prepare for the other interviewers.

The bar raiser is looking for the same things that the other interviewers are in your answers. What is that? That's a huge question – if you don't know how to answer interview questions, keep reading the book.

My advice is to just forget about the bar raiser. Or if it helps, maybe assume every person interviewing you is a bar raiser. Go into every interview expecting tough questions, and you won't be surprised. Assume each of your interviewers is going to have an unpleasant personality, a difficult accent to understand, and a list of very hard questions to answer. Prepare accordingly and you won't be surprised if someone gives you a tough time with their attitude or their questions.

Put another way, stop wasting your time trying to figure out who the bar raiser is going to be and spend your time practicing your answers.

My clients get really hung up on this bar raiser question. I get the feeling they spend more time Googling "Amazon Bar Raiser" than they do preparing. If you're doing this too, instead of writing your answers and practicing them, you're wasting your time. Are you watching endless YouTube videos about this? Do yourself a favor and stop.

I know you're worried about the bar raiser if you've done some research on Amazon interviews, but when you're spending all your time worrying about this one piece of your interview, you're probably not preparing for every interviewer to ask you tough questions.

How tough can the interviewers be?
What if someone who is or isn't the bar raiser:

- Asks you hard questions that have multiple components?

- Is arrogant and doesn't seem at all interested in you?

- Doesn't bother with any small talk at the beginning?

- Cuts you off every ten seconds?

- Types the entire time you are talking without looking at you?

- Says "that isn't a good example, do you have another one?"

- Asks you twenty follow-up questions after your first answer?

Those are all things my clients have told me have happened to them. Could you handle those situations?

For more on this topic, read the "Dealing with Difficult People" chapter.

Bar Raiser questions with examples

This is a trick section. There are no specific questions that the bar raiser will ask. They will focus on one or two principles, but that is what the other interviewers will do too.

People always ask me "What are the bar raiser questions?" Other interview coaches write articles and make videos about bar raiser questions because it's a way to get you to read their blog or watch their video. There are NO specific questions that the bar raiser asks. If you read the other sections about the types of interview questions, you will be preparing for the bar raiser as well. I keep saying, but I see more and more videos made with these titles. There is no secret list of bar raiser questions.

Hiring Meeting

After the Loop is over, the interviewers get together in a room and talk about you. It won't be on the same day as your interview but is usually in the same week, but for higher level positions it can take longer to get everyone together.

How Long Does the Process Take?

I've seen the whole process take three weeks and I've seen it take three months.

I've also seen the job get put on hold after a number of the interviews have been finished. I had one candidate who went through two interview cycles and both jobs were put on hold.

If You Don't Get the Job

If you do well but aren't a good fit for the role, they may ask you to interview for another one. If you don't do well, you can't interview at the company again for 6-12 months, but after that you are free to interview again.

They Will Be Taking Notes

Many of your interviewers will use a computer to take notes on your answers. They need the notes to write their feedback doc about your candidacy.

If you're expecting to have a conversation with your interviewer and make a personal connection, don't be upset if they don't really look at you because they're typing. Some people don't like this and it throws them off, which is why I mention it.

Chapter 3. Video Interviews

Do you have a video interview at Amazon coming up?

Video interviews, also called remote interviews, have been gaining traction with companies over the last few years, and Amazon is no exception to that. Especially with Covid-19, most Amazon interviews are now online via their video conferencing app, Amazon Chime.

Here's what to expect and what you need to know to succeed in remote interviews. I think it's safe to say that, even after Covid-19 has passed, video-based or remote interviewing is here to stay because it's cheaper and easier for companies like Amazon than flying their candidates to the office.

How to Have a Successful Video interview with Amazon on Chime

I've had Chime for a while now because I work with so many Amazon candidates and many of them have been asked to use Chime for their interviews and want to test it out with me. I already use Zoom, FaceTime, Hangouts, Skype, WhatsApp, etc., and Chime is just an alternative to those other applications. Each app brings its own set of quirks, and since Chime is less common than those others, you should set aside some time to try out the app in advance of your remote interviews.

1. Practice with Chime

To be honest, I'm not a huge fan of Chime, since I've had some problems with it. I suck at technology and normally I wouldn't dream of giving any tips in that area, but a lot of candidates are testing out Chime for the first time and my clients ask about it.

Installing Chime is easy. You'll just need to download it from the AWS site.

Once you've got Chime running, try to practice using it with a friend or family member in advance of your remote interview. Be sure to practice on the same computer that you'll be using during the interview. Depending on your operating system, you may need to grant permission to Chime to use your camera, microphone, and so on. Granting permission can lead to dialog boxes and playing around in system settings – things you don't want to be doing during the interview itself. Also, take the opportunity to test and double check that Chime is using the camera, speakers, and microphone that work best for your set up.

> Note You may be tempted to turn off your camera and interview via audio only. While you can do that, I don't recommend it. Having the camera on and facing your interviewer is a sign of respect and confidence. Don't hide from the camera!

Also, good connectivity is key. If you can, it's best to access the internet via an ethernet cable instead of wifi. If you don't have an ethernet cable, try to sit close to your wifi router, and ask your family or roommates to stop the Netflix streaming while you're interviewing.

2. Sit in a quiet place

You really need a quiet space. Taking the video interview in a crowded coffeeshop is a bad idea. Your interviewer won't be able to hear you, and it could make for a frustrating experience for all parties involved.

Turn off the TV. Turn off your phone. If you have your phone set to ring on your computer, turn that off as well. Put all pets and children out of the room. If there is loud traffic noise outside of your house go somewhere else or sit away from the window.

Don't make unnecessary noise that the microphone may pick up on or amplify. This includes typing. Use a pen and paper for notes.

You may consider muting your microphone when you're not talking, especially if there is background noise that you can't control. Just remember to unmute yourself when you start talking.

3. Look your interviewer in the eyes

Once you're familiar with Chime, you've got your computer set up, and you've found a quiet place to take the interview, you're ready for action. So how about the interview itself? My first piece of advice is to look in the camera, and not at the image of your interviewer on the screen. By looking at the camera, you're looking in your interviewer "in the eye" virtually.

If you're not quite sure how to do that, let me give you an example that might help. On the top of my monitor there are two little circles – one lights up in red when the camera is on, and the one to the left of the light is the actual camera. I need to look at the camera or else it seems like I'm not making eye contact with the person on the other side.

Your computer setup may be different than mine, so, as I said above test it beforehand. Many of my clients never look into my eyes because they look at my face on the screen instead of at the camera. This is okay in a class with your teacher, but it is *not* okay in an interview. Put a post-it note with an arrow by the camera to remind you.

4. Cheat

Here is the positive side of video interviewing – you can use a cheat sheet, and no one will never know. The video interview doesn't mean you can read your answers word for word, because it will be obvious if you do that. But it's a chance to have a small cheat sheet visible in case you need quick reminders. Why wouldn't you want to take advantage of that?

Possible cheat sheet formats:

- Notes written on paper taped to the side of your monitor
- Post-its stuck to your monitor
- Notes on your desk
- Notes on a whiteboard over your desk
- A spreadsheet open on your monitor

Use them to orient yourself at the beginning of your answer so you don't start rambling. Glance at them if you get stuck. Just don't overuse them. Don't constantly turn over sheets of paper or stare away from the camera for too long while reading your notes or let them see your eyes moving while you read.

I would use two sheets of paper, one taped to each side of my monitor, because that seems easiest to me, but I see all these different methods used.

Put a check mark by each answer after you use it so you don't repeat it more than twice.

5. Show a clean background

In remote interviews you have to worry about how you look but also how your office looks. You know how you pick out your interview outfit the night before and make sure it's clean and ironed? Now you need to plan your office setting just as carefully.

Look at the space behind you. What do you see? The interviewer should see a clean, neat space. If you're unable to create a neat space as your background, consider using the background blur feature that most video chat apps have now.

You may think I'm old-fashioned or boring or too focused on appearances and that since you're good at your job you don't need to worry about these things. The truth is we all judge people by their outward appearance in the first second we see them, and this includes during a video interview.

With these five steps out of the way, you can focus on what matters – proving to your interviewer how great you'd be at the job.

Chapter 4. The Amazon Behavioral Interview

I told you that the Amazon interview process is divided into screening and onsite interviews. This is true, but what if you're told you're having a "behavioral" interview? Where does this fall in those categories? A "behavioral interview" can fall into just about any category:

- Phone interviews
- On-site interviews (which can be on video instead of in-person)
- Technical interviews
- Non-technical interviews
- Screening interviews with the recruiter
- Screening interviews with the hiring manager
- Interviews that Amazon explicitly calls "behavioral interviews"

This is a lot of different types of interviews – which type has the behavioral questions? All the interviews, whether phone or onsite, technical, screening, or behavioral, can have small talk, basic/introductory questions, resume-related/functional questions, and behavioral questions, and also technical questions if it's a technical job.

The lines between types of interviews aren't as clear as they make them out to be, which can be helpful to keep in mind so that you aren't surprised when you get asked a type of question you weren't expecting.

Do Technical Interviews Have Behavioral Questions?

Usually technical interviews will be 80-90% technical with the rest of the time used for basic/introductory or behavioral questions. And it works the other way around too – during the "behavioral" interview you may also get some technical questions if it's a technical role.

When Should I Prepare for Behavioral Questions?

Because each interview, whether phone or on-site, may be a mix of question types, I advise you to prep for all types of questions before the first interview, even before the first interview with a recruiter. Recruiters and HR people often ask a few behavioral questions in the first interview.

Don't wait to prepare your stories for behavioral interviews until after the phone interviews are over because you think you'll need them only during the on-site interview.

Will They Ask Behavioral Questions in the Screening Interview?

Sometimes they do, yes. Usually not more than one or two, but the problem is you don't know which questions specifically you'll get asked.

Will They Ask Introductory Questions in the Behavioral Interview?

Sometimes the interviewer uses what I think of as normal interview style, which is to start with some small talk and then with the "Tell me about yourself" type intro questions, but some interviewers jump immediately into the behavioral questions with no preliminaries.

Chapter 5. The Written Exercise

Candidates for many of the jobs at Amazon receive a writing exercise that's due before their onsite interview. Amazon gives this test because candidates need good writing skills to work there.

I started out my career as an editor and then I was an English teacher, so I do a lot of work with my clients on their written exercises.

What Topic Will the Amazon Written Interview Question Cover?

The writing exercise gives you the option of answering one of two questions, and they're the same two questions for everyone:

Written interview question option one

What is the most inventive or innovative thing you have done? Describe something that was your idea, e.g., a process change, a product idea, a new metric, or a novel customer interface. It does not need to be something that is patented. Do not write about anything your current or previous employer would deem confidential information. Provide relevant context for us to understand the invention/innovation. What problem were you seeking to solve, and what was the result? Why was it an important problem to solve? How did it make a difference to the business or organization?

Most decisions are made with analysis, but some are judgment calls not susceptible to analysis due to time or information constraints. Please write about a judgment call you've made recently that couldn't be analyzed. It can be a big or small one, but should focus on a business issue. What was the situation, the alternatives you considered and evaluated, and your decision-making process? Be sure to explain why you chose the alternative you did relative to others considered.

When Is the Written Interview Question Due?

You have until forty-eight hours before your interview to submit your written exercise.

How Long Should the Writing Exercise Be?

They say four pages, but you shouldn't go beyond two and a half pages.

Essay Basics

Other things you need to know before you start writing:

- Use MS Word (rich text format).

- Copy in the question you're answering at the top of the document.

- Single space the lines.

- What font to use? Use something easy to read. Some people like Times New Roman 12 point, but I personally prefer Arial 12 point. This exercise is business writing, so keep it simple.

- Don't use bullets.

- Don't use outline format.

- Don't include proprietary information.

- Don't use headers between the sections.

How Is the Written Exercise Related to the Behavioral Questions?

If you've already been working on your answers to the behavioral questions, you may have noticed that the two written interview questions are both behavioral interview questions. These questions are asking you to tell a story about your past professional experience, like you would have to do in your interview in answer to a behavioral question.

Because the written question is a behavioral question, you can use the same information and structure that you'd use to answer the oral behavioral questions.

Writing Sample Answer Structure

Once you've chosen a topic for your writing sample, use the following format to answer it. Note that it follows almost the same structure you'd use to answer an oral behavioral question but has an added introductory paragraph before the PAR sections.

You don't need to name the sections by using headers.

Paragraph 1 – introduction

This paragraph should include an introduction to the topic and a summary of what you're going to write about, which includes the results. Also, you should provide a brief answer to the question – state explicitly the innovation or judgement call that you made.

Can be about five sentences. You don't need to get into detail, but I should be able to read this paragraph and know where you were working when you did this, what your job was, what you did (the innovation or judgement call), and the high-level results of that.

Problem section

- Corresponds to the P section (Problem) of the <u>PAR structure</u> – what is the background and the problem you were trying to solve?

- Can be more than one paragraph but not more than half a page.

Action section

- Corresponds to the A section (Action) of the PAR structure.

- Should be the longest section.

- Must say how you solved the problem you mentioned in the first paragraph – must state the innovation or judgement call. You should get to this in the first page of the essay.

Results section

- Corresponds to the R section (Results) of the PAR structure.

- What is the outcome of your judgement call or innovative idea?

- Should be at least one paragraph but can be more if necessary (and if you have some data to fill more).

Did You Answer the Question?

Make sure you answer the question. If you've chosen the innovation question, make sure to say why whatever you did was innovative. How was it new? Why did it matter to the client or the business? If you chose judgement call, you need to explain why what you did required using your judgement. Often, I will read an entire exercise and still not be clear on what the actual answer to the question is, i.e., what the innovation or the judgement call was. I know it's easy to get off track when you're writing, but your number one goal is to answer the question.

Does My Writing Need to Be Perfect?

This isn't English class in tenth grade where you had to write an essay with a five-paragraph structure and perfect syntax and grammar. Your language doesn't have to be perfect. If your English is above average or average, you should be fine. If your English is below average, you can still get the job (unless clear writing is a crucial component of the job like in PR), but you may be asked to take a writing class once you start working there. They want to make sure your emails and reports are good enough for your clients and colleagues to understand you.

Does this sound like I'm not being strict enough? I used to be an English teacher, so I actually have pretty strong opinions about language. However, I also worked in corporate America enough to know that, unless you're in PR, your language doesn't need to be absolutely perfect, including your written language.

The important thing is to use the PAR structure to keep your answer organized and clear and use the best English you can. Don't obsess about your spelling and grammar. You want to think about the question like a behavioral question. Does your answer make sense? Did you say too much? Too little? Are you answering the question?

Language Tips

In addition to what I said in the previous paragraph, your key goals language-wise should be to keep your sentences short and clear and to replace adjectives or other filler words with data.

How short is short enough? By "short," I mean your sentences should have thirty words or fewer.

One way you can do that is to eliminate any overly long words or phrases. What are those?

Unnecessarily verbose	More concise
Due to the fact that	Because
Lacked the ability to	Couldn't
For the purpose of	For
Utilized	Used
Until such time as	Until
With the possible exception of	Except

You should also replace adjectives with data because adjectives are imprecise.

Lacking data	With data
We made the performance much faster.	We reduced server side tp90 latency from 10 ms to 1 ms.
Nearly all customers	92% of Bonus-club members
Significantly better	Up 34 bonus points
Sales increased significantly in Q4.	Unit sales increased by 40% in Q4 2019, compared to Q4 2018, because of holiday promotions.

Sample Answers

I've worked with many Amazon candidates on their writing samples, and I wish I could share with you some of the best answers I've seen. However, because Amazon candidates aren't supposed to ask for help on their written exercises, I may get someone in trouble if I provide real examples. The examples that follow aren't real, but they're inspired by real answers from my clients, many of whom ended up getting the job.

Let's look at some common mistakes that I see in examples and discuss how we might avoid those mistakes in your answers.

Mistake #1 – Failing to add an introductory paragraph

I understand that it may seem tempting to follow the PAR structure and just jump right in with an explanation of the problem. However, your answer will be stronger if you take the time to include an introduction.

Your introduction is an opportunity to orient the reader (your interviewer). What's important about your story? What's the main point?

Let's look at an example of a good intro/first paragraph. Notice how straightforward and to the point this writer is in their first paragraph:

"In my current job as a Developer at Airbnb, I recently had to make a very difficult judgement call about whether to release code to production that had not been tested with our typical rigor. Because we were up against a tight deadline, I made the judgement call to deploy the code. This decision helped us meet the deadline. As a result of this success, we reviewed and changed our policies related to releasing code on production. We decided our testing guidelines were too onerous and unnecessary."

With this introductory paragraph in place, the writer can transition into the PAR structure for the rest of the essay.

Mistake #2 – Failing to provide context
Here is an example of the situation/problem step from the written exercise innovation question:

"A few months ago, I took part in a company meeting about an internal product, which I was using for consulting services. I was a user of the product, but I didn't have any formal role on this team and had little knowledge of its inner workings.

The discussion at the meeting was about how to properly roll out the product to the customers. The tech lead proposal was to release it as a downloadable and runnable application with a licensed server in the cloud. As I listened in on the team's conversation, they went into detail about installation instructions and how to implement the licensing process.

I didn't like their plan. It seemed difficult for the customer in his buyer journey with potential issues on installation, monitoring, and debugging while simultaneously introducing new customer support issues. Also, with this approach, we were losing opportunities to scale and provide valuable services to our customers."

My comments on this problem section:

There are some things that could be done better here. First, there is no background. Where was he working? What was his role? What is the internal product? Also, why was he in the meeting if he wasn't on the team?

For the problem section to work well, you must provide clear context. Anticipate and attempt to address questions that your reader may have about this situation. To address the question of why he was in the meeting, he could have simply added, "While I wasn't on the team, I was a stakeholder on the project and was included in the launch plan discussions." You want to try to paint a picture of the situation for your reader.

Let's rewrite the beginning of that problem section in a way that provides clearer context and helps the reader really see that problem from your unique point of view:

"A few months ago, I was asked to provide input on an update to one of our existing product lines. While I had no formal role on the product team, they were soliciting my input because, as an Account Executive, I sold the existing product as a part of our professional services package…"

Note that it doesn't take much to provide context. The rest of the story makes much more sense now that we know this person's role and why he was being asked to give feedback.

Here is another example of the situation/problem step from the written exercise judgement call question:

"One of my business mentors, whose opinion I value deeply, once suggested that I spend more time and a bigger budget to increase my conference and workshop attendance to enhance and diversify my pipeline of projects. As a self-employed consultant with a long project cycle from origination through execution to closing and billing, I couldn't neglect business development efforts, in particular with high-level participants. Many high-level people cannot be accessed easily, even if you come up with a referral."

My comments on this answer:

Her way of presenting this is generalized and not specific to what her situation is – what is her business? How many clients does she have? Why are conferences the answer to this problem?

Just as in the previous example, this example fails to set proper context and doesn't anticipate the readers' questions. How can we revise this example to provide context? In your own answers, give some details that will draw the reader in. Don't just speak in generalities.

Here's my attempt at a revised version of the same "situation/problem":

"At my previous job, I was struggling to build and maintain a healthy, diverse pipeline of projects. I had tried a few things to address the issue, but I wasn't gaining traction, so I went to one of my business mentors for advice. He told me that I wasn't using my budget wisely and that I should be spending more, specifically on building a pipeline by attending more conferences and workshops. I had thought that I was doing the right thing by keeping costs low. He helped me see, for high-level biz dev, sometimes you need to spend money to make money.

While using more of my budget made me uncomfortable, I pushed myself to take his advice. I built out a three-month conference schedule for me and my team, and we targeted companies and individuals that would diversify our pipeline. The approach was successful and created a model for how we built pipelines across a number of teams."

Mistake #3 – Giving too much background

Giving too much background is the opposite of Mistake #2, Failing to Provide Context. Providing too much context is just as bad as providing none. In both cases, you're failing to tell your story in an effective manner. Ask yourself, "If I were reading this story for the first time, what is the minimum amount of information I would need in order for it to make sense?"

If you find yourself wanting to provide a lot of background information, go ahead and write it all, but after you're done, try to edit it down to the essentials. If you're still struggling, ask a trusted friend or family member for help in finding the balance between providing no context and too much background.

Mistake #4 – Failing to detail your "Action"

As I wrote above, the action section is the most important section. The Action section is your place to shine. In it you must describe what action you took to address the problem.

Here is an example of an action step from the innovation question:

"I contacted each carrier to re-sign the contract with a new billing cycle and set up the account management portals to enable the report downloading features. Then I summarized the cost analysis table (cost, usage for each device, fleet, and carrier weight) and had a weekly meeting with the DevOps team to fine-tune the load-balancing algorithms to improve the cost. Finally, I worked with the customer support team to monitor complaint ticket counts to ensure no impact on customer experiences. We enacted a throttle policy adjustment weekly to balance between the overage and user experience. I also adjusted the carrier's data plan to ensure balance of demand and supply based on the device usage trend."

My comments:

While this section is a bit short (could she go through the steps in more detail?), I like that she gives herself credit for the actions she took. So often I see candidates write "we did this" and "my team did that." This section is about actions that you *personally* took to effect change and fix the problem.

However, as I mentioned, I recommend that this candidate build out the section further. For example, how did she work with the customer support team? What did she do? Did she meet with them? How did she monitor the case count?

To decide which details to discuss in the action section, consider the job opportunity. Before you write this section, reread the job description. What qualities or skills are emphasized in it? If you can show examples of how your "action" matches the qualities or skills covered in the job description (without actually referring to the job description), that's where you want to give the most detail.

Mistake #5 – Failing to describe impact

So you've set up your story with a short introduction, you've provided just the right amount of context in the Problem section, and you've detailed the steps you took to address the problem in the Action section. You're done, right?

Wrong. You must describe the impact that your action had and be specific. Data is your most important ally in this section. How specifically did your action impact the business? Did you solve an important customer problem? Great, how much new revenue did that create? Did you improve or invent a technical process? What were the proportional improvements in throughput? State the impact.

Here's an example of a Results section from the writing sample innovation question:

"I presented the document to the Finance Director, and he did not have any change requests and approved it to be used as is. He then shared it with multiple teams in the company. The Recruiting team used it to plan hiring for upcoming new site launches as it provided job titles, head counts, and contractual maximum labor costs that they could reference. The Accounting team used it to audit the payroll file to ensure labor cost billing and head counts were within contractual limit and any errors in the payroll system to be corrected as a result. The Finance team used it for budget planning and to work closely with the Accounting and Operation teams to plan any future financial needs of the company. It helped the Operations team plan ahead to pursue change orders to support business change and growth and follow up on any pending contracts that were not signed by the client yet. This document is still being used to track the contract information and status today."

Comments on this answer:

This answer is a very good Results section. It has great detail and describes the long-term impact on the business. How could we improve it? The answer, almost always, is to add some data. For example, in this case, the candidate could add how much time or person hours this new document saved, and he could even take it further and attach a dollar amount to the time savings.

Here is another example of a Results section:

"At the conclusion of the pilot period, I met with the VP and we agreed that it was too risky for us to consolidate our desktop infrastructure with a VDI vendor. I directed my team to roll back the changes, and we did so in less than two weeks.

While this may have appeared to be a failure, I saw this experience as a great success for me, my team, and the company. We moved quickly to evaluate a modern solution and gathered empirical evidence in our environment. We took a calculated risk and were able to reverse the decision when we had the information needed to make a better decision, and we were able to validate some assumptions that have proven valuable in other ways. Through this exercise, we found that VDI is a viable solution for WFH users, and we've rolled out a recently developed WFH program leveraging VDI technology."

Comments on this answer:

I found this Results section very interesting because she described how failure leads to impact on the business. She turned the failure into a "lessons learned" section, which is good. You don't have to do this but in a situation like this one, where something wasn't successful, adding some detail about what you learned can add an extra layer of insight. My one piece of advice for this candidate was, as you can probably guess, to add some data or business metrics. For her, it was easy to add that information because the program that she described brought the company six figures in new revenue. By adding that last detail, she showed the true results of her actions.

Chapter 6. How Behavioral Interview Answers Are Rated

Interviewing relies heavily on "soft skills," such as communication, problem solving, decision making, and so on. Soft skills are hard to quantify or rate because there's no universally agreed on system to rate them. However, since the goal of an interview is to pick the best candidate, interviewers need a rational system to grade candidates. To help interviewers rate candidates' responses more fairly and consistently, many companies have tried to create an evaluation system that's as standardized and quantified as possible.

Let's look at the system Amazon uses for rating candidates.

Amazon Interview Rating Scale

In Amazon interviews, the interviewers aren't using a company-wide scale to rate candidates. If Amazon is not using a company-wide scale, how do interviewers decide which candidate is best?

Amazon interviewers rank candidates in categories, which varies based on the job. Categories typically relate to the leadership principles and the functional requirements of the job.

What do I mean exactly? Let's say that the leadership principle "Customer Obsession" is an important component of the job you're interviewing for. This is common with Sales and Marketing jobs, for instance. The interviewers will pay close attention to your answers to questions related to this principle. They then discuss with each other how you did on that topic.

They will evaluate whether your skills in that category:

- Far exceed requirements
- Exceed requirements
- Meet requirements
- Fall below requirements
- Show a significant gap from the requirements

The important thing to know is that, if the job requires "Customer Obsession" and you fall into the "meets requirements" grade (or equivalent), you'll be considered average. They are looking for candidates who score higher than this.

How to know what categories you're getting rated on

One of the things that makes interviews challenging is that you aren't going to get a list beforehand of the qualities and skills that the interviewers will base their assessments on. You know the interviewers will rank you according to what they think is important for that job, but what are those things?

To be prepared, you must figure out for yourself the things they're going to ask and rate you on. The job description and your general knowledge of what the job requires are good clues of what they'll take into consideration when evaluating your ability to do the job.

Since it's Amazon we're talking about, assume that the leadership principles **most relevant for the role** will be among the categories you'll be judged on. Sometimes the recruiter will help you and tell you that the interviewers will focus on a few leadership principles. This tip can point you in the right direction, but don't assume that your interviewers won't ask you about the other leadership principles as well. It's not that I don't trust the recruiters to know what the interviewers will ask, but I...don't trust the recruiters to know what the interviewers will ask. Amazon has hundreds of recruiters, and some are better than others. Add your common sense to what they've told you.

Let's look at an example that I hope will help you get into the right mindset.

For a sales-related role, the top three leadership principles are typically "Customer Obsession," "Bias for Action," and "Deliver Results." If you're applying for a role in Sales, you can take it as a given that you'll be asked about and assessed on these principles. But in preparing for your interview, don't make the mistake of ignoring the other principles.

Besides the principles that most obviously align to the role, what other principles should you focus on to best prepare for the interview? Answering this question requires a bit of conjecture, but the following approach has helped many of my clients:

1. Start by making a list of the skills and experience that appear in the Amazon job description.

2. Search Google for other job descriptions with the same title at any company. Reviewing these job descriptions can help paint a more complete picture of what the market expects for someone in the role.

Sometimes a hiring manager won't spend much time writing a job description, so it may not be very helpful. If you look at several job descriptions, patterns will emerge that you can use to make a best guess at what the job market (and Amazon) values in candidates for the role.

3. Once you collect enough information, make a master list of requirements that are common for that job title. If the list is too long, try narrowing it down to five to seven items.

4. Now, compare this list to the complete list of leadership principles. You should be able to map between the two lists. For example, if one of the items on your list is "ability to make tough decisions," you would want to focus on "Are Right, A Lot" as one of the principles to prepare stories for.

You can read the section in the book about predicting the questions for more ideas. This chapter has some of the best guidance on interview preparation in the book, so if you haven't read it, I recommend you check it out.

What will get me the highest rating?

What exactly will get you a "far exceeds requirements" or an "A+" rating? There is no one answer to this question, but much of my book is dedicated to helping you formulate answers that will lead to positive outcomes.

You must know the leadership principles, and you must have stories about yourself that demonstrate that you embody these principles. My book includes examples to inspire you and help you tell your story.

Also, you must be well versed in the requirements for the job itself. Go through the job description carefully and form a strategy for each of the items mentioned. If it mentions a technology you've had limited exposure to, take the time to research it. Telling the interviewer that you don't have a lot of experience in an area but that you researched the topic for the interview sends a strong signal to the interviewer of your professionalism and preparedness.

Finally, while humility is generally considered a good trait in a person, the interview is no time to be humble. In an interview, you want to take credit for your accomplishments. Only you can sell yourself and your success. Help the interviewer see how great you have been and will be.

Ratings and "Level"

Related to how Amazon rates candidates is what you might call "level." That is, my clients want their answers to make them sound like more senior-level candidates. Please see the "How to Answer Correctly for Job Level" chapter for my discussion of this topic.

Chapter 7. Dealing with Difficult People

I hope all your interviewers are kind, relaxed people who ask easy questions, but let's imagine a scenario where that isn't the case. If you plan for the worst possible situation, you'll be able to handle anything without getting nervous.

One of my clients told me that he was being interviewed by three people at the same time. One person asked him a question. He answered it, but the interviewer replied, "No, that's not the right answer," and then ignored him for the rest of the hour.

That's not an easy situation. How should you handle it?

My client got upset because he assumed the interviewer didn't like him. Because he was upset, he didn't answer the rest of the questions well.

We don't know what the interviewer actually thought of my client. Yes, he didn't like that one answer. But that doesn't mean he was planning to reject the candidate from the job.

My client assumed the worst, got upset, and ruined the rest of his answers.

If he had answered the rest of the questions well, he might have gotten the job.

What Should You Do If You Have a Difficult Interviewer?

If you encounter a situation like this, an interviewer who doesn't react well to one of your answers, don't panic. If you panic, you'll answer the rest of the questions badly.

Don't assume that because one of your answers isn't exactly right or is even outright incorrect, you'll get rejected. You don't have to be perfect to get the job. Most interviewees don't give perfect answers to every question.

What Should You Do If Your Interviewer Says Your Answer Is Wrong?

Stay calm and ask if they can explain what is incorrect. Don't just move on to the next question without asking them to explain.

What Should You Do If Your Interviewer Seems Disinterested in Your Answers?

Often the interviewer will be typing while you talk (taking notes on your answers) so they won't be looking at you. Or they could simply not be particularly talkative.

There are two ways to handle this. One is to ignore it. I would probably ignore it. You could also address it - if they aren't paying attention to you, you could ask them how the conversation is going.

Chapter 8. Behavioral Interview Basics

Do you know what behavioral interview questions are? They're the type of questions that start with something like, "Give me an example of..." or 'Tell me about a time…" or "Describe an occasion when…" or "Outline a situation when…"

A popular behavioral question is, "Give me an example of when you had to deal with a difficult customer."

How Do I Know When It's a Behavioral Question?

A behavioral question often starts with "Tell me about a time…" or "Give me an example of…" or "When did you...." If you see one of these openings you have a behavioral question (also called STAR questions). Usually, people don't have problems recognizing these are behavioral questions because the question words are asking for a story.

"How" Questions Are Behavioral Questions

But what if you get asked "How do you manage employees?" or "What is your management style?" What about "Have you ever managed employees?" Most people miss that these are also behavioral questions. Even though they aren't asking explicitly for a story or example, the interviewer is expecting a story in the answer and so these are behavioral questions.

I know these questions don't sound like they're asking for an example, but you need to give one. A general answer (one without a story) isn't wrong but your answer will be much stronger if you say the general information and then add a specific example.

For example, you can say "I try to listen to what my employees are really saying and this usually helps me advise them. An example of when that worked is..." In other words, use a general answer (the first sentence) and then a specific story.

The general section of the answer can be one or many sentences but you don't want it to be so long it adds several minutes to the answer.

You never want to just give the general part of your answer because it will make your answer weaker than it could be. The point of the stories is to show you know something. You can say you know something but a story will use words to paint a picture of your experience.

If you're not absolutely sure you're being asked a behavioral question you should answer with general information + specific example, because it will make your answer stronger.

Why Do Interviewers Use Behavioral Questions?

Many people don't understand why they have to answer this type of question in their interview.

Interviewers use behavioral questions because they think that if candidates describe specific, job-related situations that happened in the past, the interviewer will get a clearer picture of the candidate's past behavior. Why do they care about past behavior? Because interviewers believe past behavior accurately predicts future performance. That's one reason these story questions are popular.

Is that true, does past behavior predict future performance? Well, that's a good question. I'm not sure that I'll do exactly the same thing in the future that I've done in the past. But that's one theory behind asking these questions.

Another reason interviewers ask behavioral questions is that interviewers believe behavioral answers show how the interviewee's mind works, how they solve problems, what they're passionate about, what they want to do, and so on. Interviewers believe that answers are a way for candidates to "think out loud" – a way to hear their thought process and the reasons they do something.

This I can believe. I do think the way we tell stories gives clues about us and about how we think.

Another reason interviewers ask behavioral questions is that hearing stories about a candidate's past jobs is a good way to judge their experience. I think this is the reason that makes the most sense to me. If I wanted to know if you knew how to do X, I'd ask you if you had done X in the past and then listen to your answer to judge how much you really knew about X.

Who Should Prepare for Behavioral Questions?

Everyone interviewing at Amazon should prepare for behavioral interview questions, even if you're applying for a technical role.

Don't assume you'll only get asked behavioral questions if you're applying for a role with managerial responsibilities. Amazon asks behavioral questions to candidates even if the job they're applying for is something that requires only sitting at a computer and talking to no one all day.

For example, I just heard from a client who was applying for a Network Engineering job at Amazon, and he told me that they only asked him technical questions (so he was happy). But I've also heard the opposite. I had a client who was also applying for a technical job there, and he said that his second phone interview (after the first short one with HR) was 1.5 hours of detailed behavioral questions, where they asked him the question and then asked for further details after he'd given his answer.

You can see that it definitely pays to prepare for behavioral questions, even if the job you're applying for is technical.

Introduction to the Amazon Leadership Principles
What are the Amazon leadership principles?

The Amazon leadership principles are sixteen ideas or values that are the backbone of the company. They are "the specific characteristics necessary for successful leadership at Amazon."

Most companies have "mission statements" but in my experience they don't take them too seriously. They're mentioned in the company marketing material but don't get used other than that.

At Amazon, these sixteen ideas are taken very seriously, not just by the senior executives but by all levels of employees.

Why are the principles important?
So why is it important for you to know the principles as you're preparing for your interview?

The Amazon leadership principles show/are the Amazon culture. During the interview, the interviewer is looking for whether you're a good culture fit, and since the culture is the same as the principles, you'll need to show how you fit in with the principles.

If you want to know more about the history of the principles and how they became so important, you should read The Amazon Way by John Rossman. It's a great book that goes in depth about the culture and the principles.

There are also countless articles online about the history of Amazon and the principles. If you're excited about working for Amazon, you've likely read quite a bit about the principles already, so I'm not going to say more about the history of them here.

All you need to know is that the principles are very important to the culture, so you must understand them before you interview.

How the leadership principles are used in interviews
During the interview you'll be judged on how well you fit into the Amazon culture. In other words, *you'll be judged on whether you are the kind of person who "lives" the principles*.

Your job in the interview is to show you are the kind of person who will live the principles.

I cannot emphasize this enough, so I'll say it again.

Your job in the interview is to show that you fit into the Amazon culture. You must show that you embody the

principles, live by the principles, and are aligned with the principles.

The big reason Amazon interviews are so challenging is that you must convincingly demonstrate that you embrace the principles, in addition to all the other normal interview stuff.

To show you *are* the right kind of person for Amazon, the person who lives the principles, you have to do a few things:

1. Read and understand the principles.

2. Memorize them, just in case they ask you which one is your favorite (a common interview question) or which are your favorites.

3. Decide which principles are relevant to the job you want (for instance, if you're not going to be hiring people, you probably don't have to worry about the "Hire and Develop" principle). We'll talk more about this later.

4. Plan stories about your past experience that illustrate each principle relevant to your job. We'll talk more about this later.

How will you be asked about the principles?
You could be asked directly about the principles or they could be mentioned indirectly. For instance, you could get a question like "What is your favorite principle?" or "How have you shown customer obsession?" or "Tell me about a time you worked with a difficult customer." You can also be asked something that doesn't seem like it's about a principle

but actually is, like "Give me an example of a time you had to communicate cross-functionally."

I put information about the leadership principles into the section about the basics of behavioral questions because the behavioral questions are where you're going to encounter the leadership principles. We'll talk more about this in greater detail later in the book.

The Sixteen Principles
Reprinted from the Amazon website.

1. Customer Obsession

    Leaders start with the customer and work backwards. They work vigorously to earn and keep customer trust. Although leaders pay attention to competitors, they obsess over customers.

2. Ownership

    Leaders are owners. They think long term and don't sacrifice long-term value for short-term results. They act on behalf of the entire company, beyond just their own team. They never say "that's not my job."

3. Invent and Simplify

    Leaders expect and require innovation and invention from their teams and always find ways to simplify. They are externally aware, look for new ideas from everywhere, and are not limited by "not invented here." As we do new things, we accept that we may be misunderstood for long periods of time.

4. Are Right, A Lot

Leaders are right a lot. They have strong judgment and good instincts. They seek diverse perspectives and work to disconfirm their beliefs.

5. Learn and Be Curious

    Leaders are never done learning and always seek to improve themselves. They are curious about new possibilities and act to explore them.

6. Hire and Develop the Best

    Leaders raise the performance bar with every hire and promotion. They recognize exceptional talent, and willingly move them throughout the organization. Leaders develop leaders and take seriously their role in coaching others. We work on behalf of our people to invent mechanisms for development like Career Choice.

7. Insist on the Highest Standards

    Leaders have relentlessly high standards – many people may think these standards are unreasonably high. Leaders are continually raising the bar and driving their teams to deliver high quality products, services and processes. Leaders ensure that defects do not get sent down the line and that problems are fixed so they stay fixed.

8. Think Big

    Thinking small is a self-fulfilling prophecy. Leaders create and communicate a bold direction that inspires results. They think differently and look around corners for ways to serve customers.

9. Bias for Action

Speed matters in business. Many decisions and actions are reversible and do not need extensive study. We value calculated risk taking.

10. Frugality

Accomplish more with less. Constraints breed resourcefulness, self-sufficiency and invention. There are no extra points for growing headcount, budget size, or fixed expense.

11. Earn Trust

Leaders listen attentively, speak candidly, and treat others respectfully. They are vocally self-critical, even when doing so is awkward or embarrassing. Leaders do not believe their or their team's body odor smells of perfume. They benchmark themselves and their teams against the best.

12. Dive Deep

Leaders operate at all levels, stay connected to the details, audit frequently, and are skeptical when metrics and anecdote differ. No task is beneath them.

13. Have Backbone; Disagree and Commit

Leaders are obligated to respectfully challenge decisions when they disagree, even when doing so is uncomfortable or exhausting. Leaders have conviction and are tenacious. They do not compromise for the sake of social cohesion. Once a decision is determined, they commit wholly.

14. Deliver Results

Leaders focus on the key inputs for their business and deliver them with the right quality and in a timely fashion. Despite setbacks, they rise to the occasion and never settle.

15. Strive to be the World's Best Employer

Leaders work every day to create a safer, more productive, higher performing, more diverse, and more just work environment. They lead with empathy, have fun at work, and make it easy for others to have fun. Leaders ask themselves: Are my fellow employees growing? Are they empowered? Are they ready for what's next? Leaders have a vision for and commitment to their employees' personal success, whether that be at Amazon or elsewhere.

16. Success and Scale Bring Broad Responsibility

We started in a garage, but we're not there anymore. We are big, we impact the world, and we are far from perfect. We must be humble and thoughtful about even the secondary effects of our actions. Our local communities, planet, and future generations need us to be better every day. We must begin each day with a determination to make better, do better, and be better for our customers, our employees, our partners, and the world at large. And we must end every day knowing we can do even more tomorrow. Leaders create more than they consume and always leave things better than how they found them.

Chapter 9. Selling Yourself in Interviews

Job interviews in the United States require that you talk about your strengths, which is also called selling yourself or self-promotion.

What Is Selling Yourself?

"Selling yourself" in an interview is the process of talking openly, clearly, and directly about your strengths – your skills, experience, and personal qualities - and explicitly stating how these strengths can help the company.

It's a form of marketing, and the product you're marketing is you.

Why Is Self-Promotion Hard for Some People?

In your daily life you don't usually get asked about your strengths or what your greatest achievement was, right? Probably not. That's not something that happens to us normally, except in interviews. Self-promotion is a skill that many of us just don't use very often.

In addition, many of us have also been taught to be humble, or not to say too much about our own strengths. Americans see selling yourself as a good thing, but many cultures, like those in Asia, think it's unfavorable to talk about how good you are.

Also, women tend to be worse at self-promotion than men. It's generally not socially acceptable, even in America, for women to brag. If you're taught at home not to brag, it's hard to learn to do it quickly before your interview.

Can You Improve Your Self-Promotion Skills?

"But I don't know how to sell myself!" is something that I hear often in my interview coaching work.

I love hearing this because I know I can help. It's easy for me, because my clients are usually smart and successful in their work, but they don't know how to express this. I can teach them how – and it isn't very hard.

Interviews are a type of communication that isn't like anything else. They're like a game you have to learn how to play. If you've never played the game before, you won't know how, but if you learn the rules and practice, you'll be able to play.

You're telling me you can learn Java or Hadoop but you can't learn to talk about your strengths? I find that hard to believe.

Why Do I Need to Sell Myself?

You've probably heard that you need to sell yourself in interviews but you might not understand exactly why.

An interview is a very short time frame. The interviewer needs to decide about you quickly. They'll know more about your skills and experience *if you tell them*.

Can't they just read your resume? Yes, your resume is a document you use for self-promotion. In your interview you need to assume the interviewer hasn't read your resume (because sometimes this is true) so you will need to tell them about your selling points, meaning your unique strengths. Even if they have read your resume, they'll remember things better if they read it and also hear it from you.

I'm sure you've known someone who got a job that you didn't think they were qualified for. You may have even seen someone in your office get promoted before someone else who was better for the role. Why does this happen? Sometimes it happens because the person is good at selling themselves to the right people.

If you don't sell yourself well, you might lose the job to someone who does, even if you would be better at the job.

Selling Yourself Isn't Being "Fake"

I'm not saying that you need to go into the interview and do an "elevator pitch" or a sales pitch.

These pitches have a bad reputation because they're what's known as the "hard sell," or being very aggressive with marketing.

That's not what I mean by marketing yourself.

That type of marketing can be too aggressive for an interview because it's one way – it's you talking (and talking). An interview should be two people talking, like in a conversation.

I think it's possible to market yourself in a natural way. I'll try to teach you to figure out what your strengths are and communicate them. That's what I think selling yourself is.

1. Make a list of your top strengths
2. Tell the interviewer what they are

Just two steps. It's possible for you to learn how to do it.

Focus On Your Core Messages

You don't want to go into an interview and tell them *everything* about yourself. Your interviewer doesn't need to know every detail.

They don't need to know about every major deal you've closed, every job you've had, every certification you have, or every single programming language you know.

In your interview you need to focus.

This is a huge problem for people.

When I ask my clients, "Tell me about your background," which is an alternative way to ask the common question "Tell me about yourself," some of them go on and on. I've heard answers to this question that were over five minutes long. This is much too long.

No one can listen for this long.

I know you're thinking that you need to give a lot of info here so the interviewer knows your skills, but the interviewer has a limited attention span.

Stick to giving shorter answers *that focus on a few core messages*.

Plan your core messages / core competencies

Core messages are your strengths. They are also known as your key selling points or core competencies.

They can be your skills, your education or training, your experience, your key accomplishments, soft skills, or your personality traits. Personality traits are a common choice to use as strengths, but I think they are a weaker choice than the other options I just gave you.

Don't forget your experience. "3 years of Java" or "10 years of biz dev" are strengths. In fact I think experience should always be on your list (for most of you – there are exceptions, like if you're a student or changing careers).

I think three to five core messages is a good . If you use more, it may get hard for you to remember and you may confuse your interviewer. But if you have six that you think are great, that's fine. My number isn't meant to be exact because everyone has a different work history.

If you're not sure what to list as your strengths, look at your resume. Your resume is essentially a document that lists your core strengths. If you've done your resume correctly, everything you want to list in the interview as your selling points should already be listed there.

Before you finalize your list, look at the job description right now and see if your core messages, or something related to them, are on the job description. If not, you need to rethink your messages. There is no reason to try to sell your interviewer on your skills if the skills don't relate to the JD.

But understand the job description first.

Sometimes job descriptions aren't written very clearly. Have you ever read one that was a page long and realized that it was the same thing written in different ways?

You might need to translate the JD into simple English before you start building your core messages around it.

I was helping a client with one recently that we both had a hard time understanding. The job was Associate Director of Sales and Operations for the Global Sales and Operations Planning and Optimization product team at Wayfair. He asked me if I could help him go over the JD to make sure he understood it before we started practicing for his interview. And it was so hard to understand I couldn't believe it (no offence Wayfair, but you need to work on your JDs). In the end the job boiled down to being a liaison between the people who tracked customer demand and the logistics people. But it did not say that in words that were easy to understand.

Before we could start practicing answers to questions we had to make sure we understood what the job was so he could target the right things with his core messages.

Examples of core messages

In case you aren't sure what I mean by core messages, here are some examples I've taken from client resumes. I've divided them by role.

Digital marketing

- Grew community from 2 million to 4.5 million, grew influencer advocate program from zero to 3,000, and drove 100,000+ webinar registrations in 2017

- Own $4+ million paid advertising budget with Krux DMP segmentation reducing CPA 31% & increasing conversion 54%

- Transformed conversion rates by 845% in trial software downloads; reduced 2300+ landing pages into 1 dynamic page

Private equity and tech investing

- Quadrilingual: fluent in English, French, Polish, and Russian

- Responsible for 300M€ spread between LP stakes in venture funds, direct equity stakes and a GP, spanning across the US, Europe, Israel and China

- Wrote blueprint for a pan-European impact investing fund in the tech area

Solutions architect

- Expertise in cloud and hybrid technologies

- AWS Certified Solutions Architect Professional

- Implementation, support and evolution of the external website for the regional airport authority hosted in Microsoft Azure leveraging IaaS and PaaS technologies

- Proficient in designing and implementing integration solutions for legacy, cloud-based and on-premise applications using different integration patterns.

Business development

- At Siemens I led the cross-divisional Smart City initiative, engaging at the CXO level with Smart Dubai and major stakeholders in the Dubai infrastructure space.

- Business development and key account management of strategic enterprise customers.

- Work with teams to create a strategic plan to grow existing customers or acquire new ones. Formulating pursuit strategies around customer needs and Aricent's unique propositions.

- Building and leading cross-functional teams that won large transformational deals.

Product management

- Hands-on product management executive with a passion to build products that delight people

- Big Data platforms, cloud, analytics, databases, middleware, integration, NoSQL and UI

- Lead product vision, strategy, and building of next-generation cloud hosting using containers, AWS and Google Cloud

- PM for large-scale text processing built on custom NoSQL with GraphDB and Lucene indexing with NLP and ML for SNA apps

These are some examples of core messages/selling points that you could use in an interview. They are all good ones, as long as the job description is calling for these qualities.

If you say that you are an expert in "Big Data platforms, cloud, analytics, databases, middleware, integration, NoSQL and UI" that's fine as long as the job description mentions at least some of these technologies or you know that the job requires them.

You absolutely need to target the job description or your knowledge of what the role requires. It can be easy to list your strengths because you're proud of having certain skills, but maybe the job doesn't require most of them.

I was just working with a client named Rajan. He was having a problem focusing his core messages. He had a lot of experience, and it ranged across sales, operations, and digital marketing roles, but he was applying for a senior level product management role. He did have the right experience, but he had so much other experience it was hard to understand he was right for the job. In his case we had to remove a lot of things he wanted to say and really focus the things he should say into a few key points.

Rank your selling points in order of most important to least important

Okay, so remember the example I just gave of some of these technologies?

- Big Data platforms, cloud, analytics, databases, middleware, integration, NoSQL, and UI

This is a great selling point (as long as you need these in the job), but should you list them first when you're talking about why they should hire you?

Well, probably yes if the job requires you to be working directly with one or all of these every day. But probably not if you're applying to be the VP of Product. In the VP role you will need to understand the technology, but it isn't the most important thing you need for the role. It might not even make your list of top five selling points.

Say the most relevant selling point first in your interview. Like I said before, frequently this might be your experience with something.

Make up general statements or examples for your core messages
You need a general statement and an example for each message.

If your core message is that you're an expert in Java, that's your general statement, so you need an example to back it up. Also, show that you're able to use that expertise to deliver results.

You can say "I'm an expert in Java. At my current job, I've written tens of thousands of lines of code for projects that reached a large, enterprise user base. As a result of my expertise, I was asked to lead the Android development team, and we shipped the company's first mobile app in under four months. The app currently has a 4.8-star rating in the Google Play store and has helped our company gain market share."

If your core message is that you are a "Hands-on product management executive with a passion to build products that delight people" that's your general statement and you need an example to back it up. Again, try to focus on results. Use numbers to bolster your case.

You can say "We just rolled out a new video player that has five thousand daily active users just two weeks after launch, up from just a few hundred users last month."

How do you use these selling points?

Once you know your core messages, you need to say them at certain points during the interview. The key is to bring in your core messages as part of your answers to the interview questions.

Where can you use your core messages?

You can use them in your responses to these questions:

- Tell me about yourself.

- Tell me about your background.

- Walk me through your resume.

- What are your strengths?

- Why should we hire you?

- Why do you want to work at Amazon?

- Why do you want this job?

- What are the responsibilities of your current job?

- In the stories you use to answer behavioral questions.

Chapter 10. Follow-Up Questions

The Amazon interview style is to ask lots of follow-up questions after the interviewee gives their initial answers.

Don't get nervous. Being asked follow-up questions doesn't mean your answer was bad. Interviewers are told to ask everyone follow-up questions. Consider these follow-up questions another part of the interview and prepare for them.

At the same time, make sure to include enough detail in your initial answer so they don't have to probe for everything. Have at least 3 minutes of details in your answer.

Follow-Up Question Format

If your first pass at the answers has to follow the PAR format, do the follow-up question answers have to as well? No. You can think of the challenge questions more like a conversation you're having with the interviewer than a traditional question and answer, so you don't need to give the full formal answer in PAR structure.

Use Real Stories

It shouldn't be hard to answer the follow-up questions if the story you're using was about a real scenario. If, however, your story isn't real, you will probably have a hard time with the follow-up questions. Some people also have problems when their story was real but they don't remember the details well enough to talk in depth about what happened.

Possible Follow-Up Questions

Here are some questions you might be asked as follow-ups.

- "What did you learn from this?"
- "What would you do differently next time?"

Questions about the beginning of your story (Situation/Task/Problem)

- Why is this important?
- What was the goal?
- What was the initial scope of the project?
- What were the challenges?
- What were the risks and potential consequences if nothing happened?
- Why did you choose this story to illustrate this accomplishment?
- What other stories can you think of that demonstrate this?
- Could you come up with an example that is more recent?

Questions about the middle of your story (Action)

- Were you the key driver or project owner?
- You mentioned that "we" did…. What exactly was your contribution versus the team?
- What was your biggest contribution?
- What unique value did you bring?
- What were the most significant obstacles you faced? How did you overcome them?

- How did you set priorities?

- How did you deal with X problem?

- How did you get manager buy-in?

- What decisions did you challenge? Why?

- How did you influence the right outcome?

- Exactly how did you approach...?

- Tell me more about...

Questions about the end of your story (Results)

- How did you measure success for this project?

- What results did you achieve specifically? (cost savings, revenue generation, volume, size, scale, percentage change, year over year improvements, time to market, implementation time, time savings, impact on the customer, the team...)

- What was the financial impact?

Chapter 11. Which Questions Will I Get in My Interview?

How will you know what questions you'll get asked?

The biggest thing that scares interviewees about their interviews is not knowing what questions to expect. Everyone is afraid that they'll be in an interview and not have an answer prepared for one of the questions.

There are so many potential interview questions you could be asked. How can you possibly know which ones to prepare for?

The first step in interview preparation is making a list of what questions you'll be asked. But how you can do that since the interviewer isn't going to tell you ahead of time?

Predicting the Questions

It's possible to predict the questions you'll be asked, and I'm going to explain it to you. If you use this method, you still might get some questions you haven't prepared for, but there shouldn't be too many surprises.

So how do you anticipate the questions you'll be asked?

How to Find Out What Question Topics You'll Be Faced With

Use the job title

The first way to find clues as to what questions they'll ask you is to look at the job title. The job title, and what you know about the job responsibilities for that job, will give you an idea of the themes of the questions and many of the exact questions.

For example, if you're applying for a managerial job, like Engineering Manager, the questions will ask things like, "Tell me about a time when you had to give someone feedback on their performance" or "Give me an example of when you mentored someone." I don't need to see the exact job description to predict these because I know that giving performance feedback and mentoring are two things that managers need to do. This doesn't mean you won't be asked questions about other topics too, but you'll definitely be asked about hiring, managing performance, developing careers, and so on, because these are core skills for managers.

You know that the Engineering Manager candidates will also get questions about the technical side of their role too, because technical knowledge is part of what it takes to be qualified for this job. They'll have to work with other engineering teams toward larger engineering goals and hold their team accountable, review and select technical vendors, set standards for best practices around coding, and/or set mechanics for how code is deployed.

When you think about the job title for the job you want, what do you know about it that might suggest topics for you? If you're applying for the job, you must have a pretty good idea of what skills it requires. These are the types of things interviewers might ask you about. Use what's already in your brain about the job to predict topics.

The second way to find clues about the questions you might get asked is to go one step further and look past the job title to job description itself. Generally, job descriptions have four parts:

1. **The Overview**

    This section will tell you the basic role you'll be doing. For example, here is the overview from a job description for an IT Sales Lead Development Representative:

    "You'll be an important member of the Sales organization, qualifying leads, profiling customers, and providing input on which sales campaigns generate the best leads. The objective is to identify and create qualified opportunities for the Education vertical, working in collaboration with your global peers, Marketing, Account Managers and the partner channel."

    This overview is giving you clues about potential questions. Every point in it could be a question. For instance, they could ask you about "When have you provided input on sales campaigns" or "What is your experience qualifying leads?"

2. **The Role and Responsibilities**

    You should read this part of the description very carefully. This section is where the everyday duties of the job are described. This is where you'll find your biggest clues about what kinds of things the interviewer will be asking.

For instance, this section might say that "You will run teams in an Agile or Scrum environment." If this is the case, then one of the behavioral questions you might get asked is "Tell me about a time you were in charge of a team that was working in Agile."

If this section lists "Update and maintain customer information within Salesforce" you may get a behavioral question about when you did this.

3. **The Qualifications**

If the role is IT Manager, one of the qualifications may be a Bachelor's in Computer Science. If you do have this degree, be prepared to discuss it. If you don't have the degree, prepare a reason that you can do the job without it.

4. **The Wish List or Desired Attributes**

Most job descriptions include a wish list of skills that aren't necessarily required but are useful. If you do have any of these, be sure to add them to your stories so it's clear that you bring something extra.

Use more than one job description

Sometimes the job descriptions are very short, and you can tell the company didn't spend much time writing it. In that case I usually search for several job descriptions – not necessarily from the same company – and then combine the info from them into one long list of requirements/skills.

Doing this will give you more to go on than a short badly written job description.

If you combine what you know about the job title with what you can see from one or more job descriptions, you should have a good list of questions to prepare for. I advise you to go through the job description and turn each bullet (and even the sentences that are written in paragraph format, usually at the beginning of the job description) into a question and then write a story for them.

Use the industry

What industry are you in? This will also give you an idea of what questions you'll be asked. If you're a Product Designer, for example, it's reasonable to expect you may get asked your opinions about current trends in product design such as design systems, design research, UX versus UI, or about your favorite tools.

Your resume

Is there anything on your resume that is difficult to explain? Are you not working now? Is there a gap between jobs? Are you switching fields? You can be sure they'll ask about those points so prepare good answers for them.

Questions for Leaders and Managers

Here are some behavioral questions that involve areas of concern for managers and leaders, such as building and managing teams, delegating effectively, executing a strategy, negotiation, and so on.

Hiring, delegating, performance management, building teams

Related leadership principles:

- Hire and Develop the Best

- Strive to be the World's Best Employer
- Success and Scale Bring Broad Responsibility

What is your management style? Why would anyone want to work for you?

How would you describe the culture on your team?

How do you motivate your team?

Tell me about your process when you're hiring for key positions. Where do you go for talent? What resources do you employ? What are the steps in the process?

What traits do you seek in candidates that signal future success on the team apart from the obvious hard skills?

How do you make sure your team is diverse?

How do you make new employees feel like part of the team?

Tell me about a time you had a low-performing individual on your team. How did you deliver feedback to this person? Did their performance improve, or did they leave the organization?

How do you coach an employee in completing a new assignment?

Give me an example of someone who was promoted one or two levels up in the organization – not just because they were a star who would naturally rise, but due to your development/coaching efforts.

How do you get subordinates to produce at a high level? Give an example.

Describe a time when you had to decide whether to award or ask for additional resources. What criteria did you use for making the call?

Tell me about a time you were able to remove a serious roadblock preventing your team from making progress.

How do you decide what tasks to delegate and which to do yourself?

Using metrics and monitoring results
Related leadership principles:

- Dive Deep
- Deliver Results

How do you use data to influence decision making?

When your direct reports are presenting a plan or issue to you, how do you know if the underlying assumptions are the correct ones? What actions do you take to validate assumptions or data?

When did you dig into a specific metric or KPI?

As a manager, how do you stay connected to the details while focusing on the strategic, bigger picture issues? Tell me about a time when you were too far removed from a project one of your employees was working on and you ended up missing a goal.

Goal setting / achieving success
Related leadership principles:

- High Standards
- Deliver Results

How do you ensure your team focuses on the right deliverables when there are several competing priorities? Tell me about a time you did not effectively manage projects and something fell through the cracks.

What's your secret to success in setting stretch goals for your team that are challenging but achievable? Tell me about a time you didn't hit the right balance. How did you adjust?

Give an example of a mission or goal you didn't think was achievable. What was it and how did you help your team try to achieve it? Were you successful in the end?

Decisiveness / speed
Related leadership principles:

- Bias for Action

Tell me about a time you felt your team was not moving to action quickly enough. What did you do?

When did you have to sacrifice quality in order to meet a deadline?

Caring about customers
Related leadership principles:

- Customer Obsession

In your opinion, what is the most effective way to evaluate the quality of your product or service to your internal /external customer? Give an example of a time when you used these measures to make a decision.

What changes have you implemented in your current department to meet the needs of your customers? What has been the result?

Taking the initiative / problem-solving
Related leadership principles:

- Ownership

Tell me about a project you and your team undertook because you saw it could benefit the whole company or your customers but wasn't being addressed.

Creating a vision / motivating a team
Related leadership principles:

- Think Big

Tell me about a time you came up with the vision for a (team, product, strategic initiative) when there wasn't a guiding vision already. What was it? How did you gain buy-in and drive execution?

Tell me about a time you had to develop a product/business model from scratch or when you dramatically changed one in a turnaround situation.

How do you ensure your team stays connected to the company vision and the bigger picture? Give an example of when you felt a team or individual goal didn't align to company strategy. What did you do?

Strategy
Related leadership principles:

- Think Big

- Are Right, A Lot

Tell me about a business model or key technology decision or other important strategic decision you had to make for which there was not enough data or benchmarks. In the absence of having enough data, what guided your choice and how did you make the call?

What are the top strategic issues you've had to face in your current role? What decisions did you end up making?

Tell me about encouraging or enabling a member of your team to take big risk. How did you balance the risk to the business with possible positive outcome for the organization and opportunity for learning for your direct report?

Relationship building
Related leadership principles:

- Earn Trust

- Customer Obsession

Tell me about a time your team's goals were out of alignment with another team on which you relied to attain a key resource. How did you work with the other team? Were you able to achieve your goals?

Tell me about a time you uncovered a significant problem in your team. What was it and how did you communicate it to your stakeholders?

Tell me about a successful working relationship you've developed with a senior leader. How did you do it? What contributed to the success?

Related leadership principles:

- Frugality

When did you challenge your team to come up with more efficient solution or process? What drove the request? How did you help?

How do you determine when to award or ask for additional resources? What criteria do you use for making the call?

Tell me how you have created organizational value through either increased revenue stream or lowering the cost structure.

Conflict mediation / negotiation / influencing others

Related leadership principles:

- Have Backbone

Give an example of when you had to support a business initiative with which you didn't necessarily agree. How did you handle it?

Tell me about a time when you pushed back against a decision that negatively impacted your team. What was the issue and how did it turn out?

When was a time you experienced competing priorities or lack of alignment? How did you resolve this?

How do you establish common ground in negotiations?

When was a time you resolved a deadlock in a negotiation?

When did you have to persuade someone in order to achieve a goal?

Give an example of when you had a disagreement with someone and then were able to arrive at a mutual agreement.

Tell me about a time when you needed to align with one or more cross-functional teams.

What is an example of a time when you had to change your communication style to suit the audience?

Quality / performance

Related leadership principles:

- High Standards

How do you seek out feedback on your team's performance? Give a specific example of how you used feedback you received on your team to drive improvement.

Can you tell me about a time when a team member was not being as productive as you needed? What was the situation? What did you do? What was the result?

Describe the process you go through to set specific targets to improve critical areas of your work/team. Please refer to a specific example.

Improving processes / change management

Related leadership principles:

- Invent and Simplify

How do you draw new thinking and innovation out of your team? Give an example of how your approach led to a specific innovation.

Tell me about a time when you enabled your team / a team member to implement a significant change or improvement.

Can you tell me about a specific metric you've used to identify a need for change in your department? Did you create the metric or was it readily available? How did this and other info influence the change?

Innovating / learning
Related leadership principles:

- Learn and Be Curious
- Invent and Simplify

Tell me about a time you challenged your team to push the envelope and go beyond existing standards and expectations.

Give a specific example of where you realized your team had not been as effective as it could have been. What feedback mechanisms did you use?

When did someone on your team challenge you to think differently about a problem? What was the situation and how did you respond?

What is an example where your team was unable to achieve a goal or milestone, but the information gathered during the project enabled future success.

Tell me about a time when a member of your team contributed significantly to a project outside the scope of their role. What motivated you to encourage their participation?

Collaboration
Related leadership principles:

- Earn Trust
- High Standards
- Deliver Results

What was a situation when you collaborated with a business leader outside your function and gained support?

Talk about the most complex cross-functional initiative you've led.

Managing ambiguity
Related leadership principles:

- Are Right, A Lot

What was a time you made a complex decision with limited data or information?

When was a time you needed to define the scope of a project on your own with limited support?

Describe a situation when you didn't understand a problem. How did you approach it and solve it?

Question Topics by Seniority Level

Interview question topics (and the leadership principles related to them) will change as you go up in your career level.

Whether you're in finance like in the example I'm going to use here or in some other field, the lower-level jobs are usually more focused on collecting data and reporting on it or doing something technical than the higher-level jobs, which are more focused on managing teams, strategy, and monitoring results.

Knowing this can help you know where to focus your preparation efforts. If you know you're applying for a lower-level job, you should start by creating stories for the principles you'll probably be asked about first.

A job like Financial Analyst or Senior Financial Analyst should focus on:

- Diving into the data/doing research. What does the data tell you? The "Dive Deep" principle.

- Quality. Are your deliverables excellent? The "High Standards" principle.

- Your ability to take action. Can you act quickly versus getting stuck in analysis paralysis waiting for someone else to make a decision? The "Bias for Action" principle.

A job like Finance Manager (a level up from Senior Financial Analyst) should focus on:

- Judgement. Do you know how to make good decisions? The "Are Right, A Lot" principle.

- Can you work with other people successfully? Are you an indirect influencer on other lines? Do you communicate well? The "Have Backbone" and "Earn Trust" principles.

- Are you innovative? Do you look for new and better ways of doing things for you and your customers? The "Invent and Simplify" principle. (Although this one can also be very important a level down as well.)

- Do you know how to build to scale and simplify processes? "Invent and Simplify."

- Do you know how to measure the success of your own work and also work that you've delegated to others? "Dive Deep."

These skills focus on the bigger picture more than just looking at the data for one project and equally on people skills and technical skills.

A job one more level up like Senior Finance Manager or above that Director of Finance should focus on:

- Hiring and developing talent. The "Hire and Develop" and "Strive to be the Earth's Best Employer" principle.

- Do you know how to speak up if you see the wrong decision being made? Can you make unpopular decisions? Can you negotiate in a way that all groups are happy with the result? The "Have Backbone" and "Earn Trust" principles.

- Looking at the big picture and seeing how pieces fit together and making long-term plans. The "Think Big" principle.

- Measuring the success of your projects and of the work that your teams are doing. "Dive Deep."

At the higher level you should also be able to answer questions about the concepts from the lower-level jobs too. Just because you've moved up a level doesn't mean you can forget what you used to know. Although you may not be doing those tasks anymore, the people you're managing probably are and you'll still need to be able to judge their work.

Notice that some of the principles overlap levels. That's okay. Your job will be different as you move up, but some of the tasks will be similar. For instance, you may need to dive deep at all levels, but on a higher level you'll be measuring more than just your own projects' success. The task is still the same – doing research – but you aren't researching exactly the same things from level to level.

Because answering for job level is a key concern for so many of my clients, I cover the topic in more detail in the chapter titled "How to Answer Correctly for Job Level."

Chapter 12. Using Stories

Use stories to answer behavioral questions

Behavioral questions aren't questions you can answer "yes" or "no" to. If you're asked to "Describe a time you failed at something," you can't just say, "Yes."

To answer behavioral questions, use a story. Some people think of these questions as "story questions."

The story you use as your answer should be about something that happened to you at work (unless you don't have much or any work experience) that shows the skills you've been asked a question about. Don't use personal stories. If they ask you about a time you took a risk, don't talk about the time you decided to accept a new job even though you didn't know how it would turn out or it was offering you less money. The point of asking you these stories is to see how you operate at work, not in your personal life.

Why does storytelling work in interviews? It works because the stories are giving information to show that you can do the job. Stories help you connect with the interviewer on both the logical and emotional level. The goal isn't to entertain, but to help the interviewer understand you so you can ultimately get the job.

If you want some more help writing your stories, keep reading. By the end of the book, you'll understand why you need to write stories and how to write good ones.

How Many Different Stories Do I Need?

You will usually get asked between two and six behavioral questions in a one-hour interview. Because you can't know exactly how many you'll get asked, you should prepare for the higher number, six. Also, even if you get asked only one question, you don't know which one it will be. You need to prepare enough answers to make sure you have a story that will work for that particular question.

Fifteen to thirty is a good number of stories.

If you have fewer than fifteen you could be in trouble, but if you have more than thirty it's hard to remember them all.

I said to prepare fifteen to thirty stories, but I don't know the exact number of behavioral questions they'll ask you. Each interview is different. If you have five, six, or seven interviewers, and they each ask you five behavioral questions, that's thirty-five questions. What if you have five interviewers and they each ask you three behavioral questions? That's fifteen questions.

I've had clients tell me they've gotten six questions in a one-hour interview. I've also had clients tell me they've gotten one, or more than six.

That's why my answer is fifteen to thirty stories, because it's my best guess.

Create a Pool of Stories and Then Tailor Them to Fit Specific Questions

Create a pool of stories – between fifteen and thirty – and then tailor the stories for different questions depending on which ones they ask you.

What do I mean by tailoring a story for whatever question you get asked? What if you have two stories you've planned to use for ownership questions, but you also have two customer related stories. You use your two ownership stories, but then you get asked a third ownership question. What do you do? You could not answer the question, or you could take one of your customer stories and use it to answer the ownership question if you change the wording a little. The latter is obviously the best choice because it's best if you answer all the questions.

Altering, or tailoring, an answer quickly isn't easy and can take some practice. What you want to do is create a group of stories, and then spend your prep time practicing tailoring a story to work for different questions. If you practice tailoring stories, you will get good enough so you can adapt them quickly, after you hear what question, you need to answer.

You can take a basic story and alter it to fit whatever question you get asked. If you get asked a customer question, you'll focus your answer on talking about the customer. If you get asked an ownership question, you'll focus your answer on how you took charge. If you get asked a successful project question, you'll focus your answer on the successful outcome. And so on.

How to Track Your Stories

As you know by now, you'll need stories you can use for your answers to behavioral questions. If you've started practicing answering these questions, you've probably realized thinking of good stories and then picking the right one to answer each question isn't that easy.

How can you track your stories and pick the right one quickly in your interview?

Think about this problem – what if you have 30 stories? How will you know which is the best for a particular question without reading them all, which you won't have time to do in your interview?

I used to think writing them down in a spreadsheet was good enough, but I realized a lot of people who created spreadsheets were having trouble getting to the right answer fast enough.

How do you create a story tracking system that lets you easily and quickly select the best accomplishment?

I think the best way to help you pick a story quickly is to give your story a short name that has keywords in it. This way you can find it quickly.

In your spreadsheet, or whatever document you're using to compile your stories, write down the keyword the story is about. Then write down the story – I advise using bullet points only, or else you might accidentally memorize it word for word.

Once you've gotten further in your practice and know the stories well enough, you can make a smaller version of the spreadsheet with only the keywords on it or the keywords with a few bullet points.

In interviews you can keep the condensed version with you, on your monitor or on paper on your desk or taped to your monitor, so you can scan it if you get stuck.

Can I Write Your Stories for You?

If you're planning to work with me, I can definitely help you with your stories, but I can't think of them for you because I don't know what you've done in your past jobs.

I get a lot of requests to write answers for clients but that's impossible for me to do. I can help you brainstorm ideas for stories, because I've heard so many of them, and I can help you improve your stories, but you're going to have to write the basic outline and think of some details yourself.

Be careful about buying answers that someone else wrote. You can copy the structure of someone else's answer, but if you copy more than the structure your answer won't sound natural.

If you work with me, you'll end up with a portfolio of answers that you can use for the behavioral questions and if you work with another coach you should end up with the same thing.

What Makes a Good Story?

A good story makes you seem like a good candidate for the job. So the main thing your story needs to do is show you have skills that relate to the new job.

How do you do that?

- Pick the right topic to talk about
- Tell the story clearly using the STAR/PAR technique
- Include enough details so your answer is around three minutes

Most of this book is about how you write good stories. I'll get into answers for specific questions later and I'll also talk about the STAR/PAR method later.

How to Create Your Stories: Brainstorming

To answer behavioral questions, you'll need to use a story. How can you think of stories?

How to think of ideas for your stories

I have a bad memory so it's hard for me to remember what I did at past jobs. If you have a similar problem remembering what you did at work, here are some tips that might help you think of material you can use for stories:

- Look through your old files or emails.

- Ask past colleagues about past projects.

- Ask past colleagues what they think you did well.

- Look through your old performance reports.

- Look at your resume – if you wrote it correctly, you'll have your past projects and successes written on it.

- If you still can't remember anything, look at the job description (or your old job descriptions) for clues. What do they want you to be able to do – have you ever done that?

You can also think of things that happened in the past in terms of accomplishments. What successes did you have? Once you've written down the major ones, think of anymore, even if they weren't quite as substantial. If you don't have a great achievement from the workplace, think back to internships or time in school.

Hints to help you think of accomplishments or failures:

- Did you think of an idea that got used?

- Were you creative in some way?

- Did you show leadership?

- Did you set a goal and accomplish it?

You'll probably be asked about successes in your interview so it's useful to think of as many success stories as possible.

You'll need stories about mistakes or failures too. Try to think of failures that you learned something from, since you'll need to include what you learned as part of the story.

Plan stories based on the functional competencies
You can plan your stories starting with functional competencies, also known as job requirements. If you need SQL skills for the job and you can think of a story about how you did something successful with this skill, you can make a story about that.

Go through the job description and look for all of the points they're looking for in a candidate. This is the same process that you should have used to predict what questions they'll ask you.

Each item they're looking for is something you may have done in the past. If you have, think of a story about it.

How to get enough details for your stories
The first phase of writing a story is thinking of an idea, and the second phase is thinking of details.

Once you have your idea, write as much info as you can about it. Aim for at least a page of writing. If you can remember any details, write them down. You can also talk to someone who worked on the project with you for more details.

Don't edit yourself before you write. Don't worry about structure. Just write down some notes in any kind of form. If you write down everything, you can think of without worrying about whether it's good you'll think of the most details.

Here are some prompts you can use to think of details:

- Where was I when this happened? Where was I working? Who did I work for or with?

- What was the situation? What was I doing related to the situation?

- How did I feel? Was I stressed? Was I happy?

- What actions did I take? Why did I do this?

- What happened in the end? Did I learn something from this?

Once you've remembered everything you can about the incident, then you can extract the best info and turn that into a story.

Don't use personal stories
The story should be about something that happened to you at work (unless you don't have much or any work experience) that shows the skills you've been asked a question about.

Don't use personal stories, even for the "risk" question – for some reason everyone wants to use a personal story for this. It's okay to use a personal story if it's about starting your own company, but that's the only personal story that's okay to use.

Story Structure

The STAR method

In the answers to behavioral questions, you need tell a story about your past experience.

The STAR technique was invented to help you give good answers to these behavioral questions by telling clear stories.

STAR isn't just used by Amazon; it's a standard format for answering behavioral questions. There are other formats but STAR is the most common so your answers will work for other companies too if you happen to be interviewing in more than one place.

What is the STAR technique?

The STAR technique is a common system used to answer behavioral interview questions. (You can't really use it for questions like "Tell me about yourself.") It provides a structure for you to remember so that you include the correct data in your answers.

These are the four steps of the technique:

> **S** – Situation
> **T** – Task
> **A** – Action
> **R** – Result

Let's look at each of those steps in detail.

Situation/Task

Describe the situation/task you faced and the context of the story. Answers the questions: Where did this occur? When did it happen? Why is it important? What was your job?

Action

What actions did you take? Answers the questions: What did you personally own? How did you do it? Who else was involved?

Results

How did you measure success for this project? What results did you achieve? In your results consider the following:

- Cost savings, revenue generation
- Quantify to understand volume, size, scale
- Percentage change, year over year improvements
- Time to market, implementation time, time savings
- Impact on the customer, the team
- Quality improvements

If you get asked a behavioral question, answer by going through the letters in order. First give the **S** part (explain the basic situation). Then give the T (what was your job/task in this situation?) Then **A** (show what you did). Last, give the **R** (outcome).

The goal is to focus on all of the steps. Don't skip a step.

S/T – After I got promoted, I realized that we had more projects than originally planned and I would need more product managers to complete them. Hiring was my responsibility, so I needed to decide how many to hire.

A – I charted our planned projects and then decided how many people I thought I needed. I used our records as well as my own observations. I came up with the number of people and then asked my colleagues for their opinions. Once we had a final number I worked with recruiting to interview candidates and eventually hired the right number of people.

R – Now we're adequately staffed, and the work is going well.

> *Tip:* This candidate uses the right structure, but notice that the Results sections lacks metrics. If possible, pick an example where you can use numbers in your results. For instance, "And we made 5% more this quarter," or "My sales numbers are up 25% over last year." Numbers, particularly financial metrics, make the results more impressive.

Sample answer – "Tell me about a time you had a difficult situation with an employee."

S/T – I recently had an employee, one of my product managers, who was not performing well. The people she worked with were complaining about her attitude and the executives were complaining about the quality of her work. They wanted me to fire her but I wasn't sure that was the right thing to do.

A – I talked to HR and the executive team, and we decided to collect the evidence about her performance in a document and then present it to her. I did this. During her review, she was very angry and blamed her problems on the company structure. In the end, we decided that we would work closely together for 60 days to improve her performance.

R – My plan was successful in that her performance did improve (as well as her attitude). I'm not happy with the amount of time I have to spend with her, but I hope that by spending the time mentoring her now I will end up with a good product manager who can work independently of me.

Do I actually need to use a structure in my answers?

Interviewers are given instructions from Amazon on how to evaluate answers. The first part of the instructions tells them to evaluate the example using STAR - "Stories should have a beginning (Situation/Task), middle (Actions), and end (Results)."

Do you have to use STAR? Not necessarily. If your story has a beginning, a middle, and an end it should be clear.

PAR not STAR

I hope you now understand STAR, but what is PAR?

Many people who know the STAR method find it confusing to use because the S and the T steps seem so similar. If you have no idea what I'm talking about you can skip this section and keep using STAR.

So, the "situation" and "task" steps in STAR, they seem kind of similar, right? Yeah, they do. I've had many clients ask me to explain the difference to them.

To save everyone from confusion, I've started teaching my clients to use "PAR," which is the same as STAR but combines the **S** and the **T** steps.

Why **P** instead of **S**? **S** and **P** are the same thing – situation, problem, issue – it doesn't really matter what you call it, it's the same thing.

> **P** – Problem/situation/issue
> **A** – Action (what did you do?)
> **R** – Result

Now use the letters as a structure to tell your story.

Will the interviewers notice that you're not using STAR? No. Absolutely not. Your answer will sound the same, but it will probably be clearer because the structure is simpler (and you understand it better).

A good sample answer for a common behavioral question
This is a common behavioral interview question that you might be asked in an interview. I've marked it with the PAR sections so you can see the structure of the answer.

Give an example of a goal you reached and tell me how you achieved it.

P – Last year at my quarterly review my boss explained to me that I needed to improve my public speaking skills, since I'm in marketing and give presentations to my colleagues and clients frequently. He said that I speak too softly and too quickly and don't explain my ideas clearly.

A – I didn't know how to get better at this, so I hired an executive coach. I worked with her for a month, and then joined a group of her former clients who meet once a week to give speeches in front of each other. With her help and all of their comments and support, I learned to see what my weaknesses were.

R – After working on my skills for several months, I could see that my presentations were better. At my next review, my boss agreed. Now I'm continuing to meet with the group so that my skills keep improving. I want to be even better than I am now so that I give excellent presentations.

Why is this answer good?

It talks about a skill that will be relevant in the job she is applying for. It follows the PAR structure. It keeps to the details that are needed but doesn't add more.

Try to do the same things when answering your questions.

SOAR versus STAR versus PAR

Which structure should you use to answer behavioral questions?

You may have noticed that there are quite a few different acronyms out there relating to behavioral question answer format. Each one is a different template to use to answer behavioral questions. Which one is the best?

I want to explain to you what the idea is behind these structures/acronyms so you can make your own decision.

On the most basic level all the formats are trying to make it easier for you to answer behavioral questions. And hey, that's great, because it does make it easier to remember what to include in your story if you remember an acronym.

But why does one person say to use STAR and one person say to use SOAR, etc.? If I don't listen to the right person, will I fail my interview?

I understand the anxiety you're feeling, because the people writing about this topic don't make it easy. When someone says to use STAR, for instance, they usually say "this is the structure you need to use to answer these questions." They don't say "this is one of many possible structures you can use if you want to." It's always presented as if this were the best and only option. But the truth is, you have quite a few choices.

But if I use the wrong one, will my answer be wrong? No, and this is why: these structures are essentially the same.

SOAR
S – Situation
O – Obstacle
A – Action
R – Result

STAR
S – Situation
T – Task
A – Action
R – Result

STARL
S – Situation

T – Task
A – Action
R – Result
L – Learnings

STARI
S – Situation
T – Task
A – Action
R – Result
I – Impact

PAR
P – Problem
A – Action
R – Result

So as you can see, they have similar but not always identical sections (the letters). Let's do a comparison so you can see the actual differences.

Situation / Problem

For the first section, you've got S or P, Situation or Problem. And what does that mean? State the problem, or issue, or situation. It doesn't matter what you call it, it means the same thing.

Task / Obstacle

For the second section, you've got task or obstacle (Or nothing). Okay, which is better? Well, think about the first section. Let's do an example. What is the problem you are talking about? Let's say the problem is that I'm the IT Manager for my department and one of the computers is broken and it needs to be fixed today but I don't have anyone free to fix it. Okay. Well, so what is my task? Fix the computer or get someone to fix it. In my opinion, this has already been stated in the problem so we don't need a task section. What is my obstacle? Broken computer? No time? No resources? Again, already stated in the problem.

If you are stating your problem or situation correctly, you will be including the information about task.

Here's another example in case you don't see what I mean. Your problem is that you have a report due for your client in 5 days. Well, the task is that you need to finish the report in 5 days. Even if you don't say this out loud, the task is implied in the problem statement. A good problem statement will be very explicit about the issues.

Obstacle is whatever might keep you from fixing the problem or completing the task. Again, in my opinion, if there is an obstacle it should be part of the problem statement. In the first example I gave, if your obstacle is that everyone in your department is out sick that day, you should say that in the problem. In the second example, if your obstacle is that the client won't respond to you to give you the information you need to include in your report, that should be part of the problem statement.

If you keep forgetting to state the task or obstacle in your answers, you can use the acronym that will remind you, but for me the T and O are part of the problem so I always mention them.

Action
The action step is included in all the structures.

Result / Impact

You obviously need an ending to every story, which is why we have the results section. Do we also need an impact section? Well, to me they are the same. If you see a difference between result and impact you can use both sections, but I don't see a difference. If you have a good results section that is enough.

Lessons learned

In some questions, like the mistakes/failures, the learning section should always be included. In other questions it's up to you whether you want to talk about what you learned. Sometimes that's a natural part of a story and sometimes not. I find it excessive to always include this section in every answer.

Chapter 13. Tailoring Your Stories to the Principles

Which leadership principle is this question asking me about?

If your Amazon interviewer asks a behavioral question, how will you know which leadership principle they're asking about?

If your interviewer asks, "When have you taken a risk?", do you know which principle this question falls under? How quickly did you figure it out?

How to connect the leadership principles to the questions is a topic my clients ask me about frequently. Many of my clients make spreadsheets with their stories and map them to the associated principles, which I think is a great organizational approach. But – what if you take the time to make a spreadsheet, and yet you still can't remember the correct principle once you're in the interview?

I used to tell my clients to memorize the most common questions for each principle so that they would immediately know which principle to target in their answers. While I continue to believe this comprehensive approach is the best way to prepare for an interview at Amazon, it can take a lot of time to become familiar with the sixteen principles – time that you may not have if your interview is coming fast.

Shortcut

I'll give you a shortcut: just make sure your answers – to any question – demonstrate excellence or high performance.

How can I say that? How can you answer the question if you don't know which principle the interviewer is asking about? Isn't the whole goal of the interview to show that you fit the principles? Yes, that is the goal of the interview. But you can still demonstrate you're a good fit for the principles without knowing which exact principle the interviewer is asking about. How? Let's think about it.

Consider the principles as a whole

Put together, what is the general idea behind the principles? If I had to choose one word to describe the primary theme across all principles, I would pick "excellence," a trait found in all high-performing individuals. Excellence is apparent in every principle.

For example, consider "Customer Obsession," which is the first principle and is covered in detail in the next section. "Customer Obsession" means caring deeply about the customer and doing excellent work for them. So if you get a question like, "How do you develop relationships with clients?", you must demonstrate in your answer that you have a process for forming relationships with customers that is extraordinarily good. We'll go over some specific examples when we examine the principle in detail.

Questions about "Customer Obsession" are easy to spot because they usually include the word "customer." What about something less obvious? Consider a common Amazon interview question such as, "Tell me about a time you had to go above and beyond." Which principle is this question referencing? It might be "Ownership" or "Highest Standards" or "Bias for Action," but it doesn't really matter. You don't have to know which principle it references to craft a terrific answer. You simply need to show in your answer that you've taken the initiative to do something outside of your normal routine and done an excellent job of it. If in your answer you're successful in demonstrating your excellence, you're showing "Ownership" and the other principles it relates to as well.

Use the shortcut instead of panicking

I recommend you memorize answers for each principle, but as I said before, that can take time. In an interview situation, you may (and probably will) be asked a question that doesn't map cleanly to one of the principles, or does map to a principle but you just can't remember which one, or maps to more than one. If that happens, don't panic. If you're asked, for example, about going "above and beyond" and you don't remember which principle(s) the question relates to, don't waste time fretting about the exact principle. Instead, focus on answering the question in a way that demonstrates your excellence. Show how you refused to accept the status quo (even when others around you did accept it), performed beyond expectations, and strove for excellence (even if you didn't completely succeed).

In suggesting this approach, I don't mean to be overly simplistic. I mention it because I see so many of my clients go to an interview, get stuck on what specific principle they're supposed to be talking about, panic, and give a bad answer. When the interviewer asks a question, people mentally run through all the principles and wonder which one to address. That's a waste of time. Answering questions quickly and confidently is important.

So once again, before the interview, ask yourself what the principles as a whole mean. Why do they exist? What are the interviewers really looking for?

What do people always look for in any interview? They're looking for someone who demonstrates excellence. You need to be that kind of person. Are you the type of person who will always bend over backwards to help the customer, who will always do more than is required, and who performs well without supervision? That's excellence, and that's what they're looking for.

Pretend you're not even interviewing with Amazon. How would you answer the question if the principles didn't exist?

If you're reading this chapter and identifying with the problem I'm talking about, you may be obsessing over the principles too much.

Am I overanalyzing?

I get this question a lot from clients who've put a lot of time into their story spreadsheets. Are you overanalyzing? Well, not necessarily. If I had an interview coming up for my dream job, I'd be spending a lot of time prepping too.

However. Step back for a second. You may be fixating too much on the idea that there are these principles you must adhere to. Think about the Amazon culture as a whole. Or step back even further and think about American tech culture as a whole. Do you fit in with that? Forget the individual principles and figure that out.

What is American tech culture? I talked about excellence before, but can we get more specific? Do your answers show you will do what it takes to succeed (as long as it's legal and ethical) – whether succeeding is creating a great product, or giving your customer what they want, or whatever else? Will you always work hard and fight for your ideas if you think they're good? Are you highly analytical, data centric, and competitive?

Focus on showing excellence

Do you keep researching and researching the principles, reading more and more articles, and watching more and more videos trying to understand them? That's a sign you may be going overboard on the principles. Focus instead on creating stories that show you're a high performer in your area. Focus on your own excellence.

Stories for the Sixteen Leadership Principles

Customer Obsession

The first and perhaps most important Amazon leadership principle is "Customer Obsession."

I recommend that everyone, no matter what role you're interviewing for, prepare answers for the "Customer Obsession" questions. This is truly Amazonians' favorite leadership principle, so you need to be able to show you understand it and take it seriously.

This is how Amazon explains the principle:

Leaders start with the customer and work backwards. They work vigorously to earn and keep customer trust. Although leaders pay attention to competitors, they obsess over customers.

What does this principle mean? It means that most companies are competitor-focused and want to make sure they don't fall behind but Amazon, on the other hand, looks at their entire business through the eyes of the customer.

If you're obsessed with customers, you will:

- Collect data on and deeply understand your customer's needs and wants
- Ask yourself, "Is what I'm working on helping my customers?"
- Rigorously pursue customer feedback
- "WOW" your customers
- Provide products and solutions that exceed customer expectations
- Remove steps in your process that don't add value
- Treat your customers like they're #1

What are examples of "Customer Obsession" questions in Amazon interviews?

I've explained what the principle is about, so now how will this principle show up in your interview? Will your interviewer ask, "Are you obsessed with customers?" They might ask about the principle in this straightforward way, but the questions are typically more subtle than that. Here are some of the ways you may be asked about this specific principle:

- When you're working with many customers, it's tricky to deliver excellent service to all of them. How do you prioritize the different customer needs?

- Tell me about a time you handled a difficult customer. What did you do? How did you manage the customer? What was her or his reaction? What was the outcome?

- Most of us at one time have felt frustrated or impatient when dealing with customers. Can you tell me about a time when you felt this way, and how you dealt with it? What was the outcome?

- When was a time when you had to balance the needs of the customer with the needs of the business? How did you approach the situation? What were your actions? What was the result?

- Give me an example of a change you implemented in your current team or organization to meet the needs of your customers. What has been the result?

- Tell me about a time a customer wanted one thing, but you felt they needed something else. What was the situation and what was the action you took?

- Tell me about a time you used customer feedback to change the way you worked. Why did you take the action you did? What was the outcome?

- Tell me about a time you had to compromise in order to satisfy a customer.

- How do you get to an understanding of what the customer's needs are?

- How do you develop client relationships?

- How do you anticipate your customers' needs?

- How do you "wow" your customers?

- When do you think it's ok to push back or say no to an unreasonable customer request?

These questions do not use the phrase "Customer Obsession," but they're asking about the idea behind the principle, which is caring about customers and how you make customer experience a priority.

How to answer "Customer Obsession" questions
You need to tell a story, which you can structure using the PAR technique (Problem/Action/Result). I cover this structure earlier in the book.

As with the other principles, use a story from your past work experience to answer the "Customer Obsession" questions, even if you get asked "How do you wow your customers?" or another question beginning with "how." "How" questions tend to confuse people because they seem like the interviewer is asking you to answer more generally. In fact, to give a strong answer, you need to talk about something specific. Answer this and other "how" questions with something like, "I try to go above and beyond to serve my customers" [general statement about how you approach dealing with customers]. For example, once last year I had to..." [a specific story]. In other words, don't give just a general answer that describes your personality or work habits. Be sure to include a specific example about something that happened to you at work that involves helping the customer.

In your interview answers, show that you understand your customers and their needs. You don't want to sound like someone who just does the tasks assigned to you as part of your job without ever taking a step back to understand who uses the product or service.

What if you consider your boss or another internal stakeholder, like a business unit or department, your "customer" because you are doing your work for them? This might be the case if you are in a role like Finance, etc. That's fine. You can use stories where you are showing that this internal department is your customer.

Avoid clichés such as "the customer is always right." Showing "Customer Obsession" doesn't mean you always do exactly what the customer asks. True "Customer Obsession" is about understanding the problem behind a customer request. Solving that problem might include something the customer never even imagined.

For inspiration, consider reading about Jeff Bezos's obsession with customers. A quick Google search on the topic will return many examples. I like this article on Inc., which quotes Bezos as saying, "What matters to me is, do we provide the best customer service. Internet shminternet. That doesn't matter." Note how, in that interview, Bezos connects opening new warehouses and hiring new employees back to servicing customers. Everything Amazon does is about the customer.

Sample answers for customer obsession questions

Question: Tell me about a time you handled a difficult customer. What did you do? How did you manage the customer? What was her/his reaction? What was the outcome?

Here is an answer given by a **Sales Manager**:

"When I was a Sales Manager at X, we had a group of unhappy customers. We'd sold them a weed killer that hadn't worked well. As farmers, they relied on the weed killer, and they were threatening to take their business to our competitor. I had to try to keep them as customers. I knew retaining them would be hard because our product had been defective and had cost them money. I had a meeting with all of them where I listened to their complaints. I listened to each of them and responded calmly. I explained to them what had happened, which was definitely our fault, and apologized. In the end, they agreed to give us one more chance, even though I couldn't offer them a refund, since I didn't have the ability to do that."

This answer uses the PAR structure and is therefore easy to follow, but it's **lacking in detail**. In general, you want your answers to be about 3-4 minutes long. This answer is about half that. Let's revise it. We'll keep the PAR structure, but we'll add some more detail to demonstrate the candidate's "Customer Obsession." We can also emphasize skills that will be relevant to the job she is applying for – dealing with unhappy clients, client communication, and conflict management.

Here's the revised answer:

Problem: When I was a Sales Manager at X, we had a group of 50 unhappy customers. We'd sold them a weed killer that hadn't worked as advertised. The product worked to kill weeds, but not as well as we said it would (not 100% of the weeds died). As farmers, they relied on the weed killer, and they were threatening to take their business to our competitor. I had to try to keep them as customers. I knew retaining them would be hard because our product had failed to deliver and had cost them money.

Action: Relationships were especially important to these customers, and the primary component of a customer relationship, in my experience, is trust. By selling them a faulty product, I had betrayed that trust. Repairing it would not be simple and would require a lot of time, time that I would otherwise be using to sell to other customers. But I thought the time would be worth it because my reputation was on the line, not to mention the reputation of the company.

Restoring trust is about admitting you were wrong and, above all, listening. I had a series of meetings with the farmers, where my only goal was to listen. Not to try to sell to them. Not to promise we'd do better. Just listen. I first met with them as a group, and then I met separately with several of them. I listened to each of them and responded calmly. I explained to them what had happened, which was definitely our fault, and apologized. In the course of our conversations, the farmers became less frustrated with the situation and were ready to look ahead.

Result: While I didn't have the ability to give them a refund for the defective product, in the end, they agreed to give us one more chance. I knew that I still needed to deliver a quality product to completely restore trust, but not losing them as customers was a major victory.

I've added a few things to this revised version of the story. First, there is more detail about the problem, i.e., the product had not worked as well as advertised. Second, the Action section needed a lot of work. It was too short. The Action section should typically be the longest part of your answer, and it's your place to show your skills. In this revised version of the story, the Sales Manager shows that she understands what's important to the customer (relationships), and she devises a strategy around that. She implies that fixing the customer relationship will cost her money in the immediate term ("time that I would otherwise be using to sell to other customers"), but she does it anyway because she's thinking about the longer-term implications. This revised version is much better than the original.

Question: How do you get an understanding of what the customer's needs are?

Here is an answer given by **a Senior Digital Product Manager**:

"I use quantitative and qualitative approaches. Quantitative is looking at data to derive insights. Data can be what are customers doing when they use your product and, if you're working on a digital product, you could use an approach like web analytics. With qualitative approaches, you can simply ask them about their needs about how they use your product, but a better way is to immerse yourself into their problem space and ask where does the product fit into their daily life today? For example, in looking at my top customers, in terms of the customers most engaged on my platform, I can see that content about IT certification is very popular. As a result, we started doing online trainings and certifications. So instead of just a course or video, we do live trainings now. Those turned out to be really popular. So it seems that anything we give them in terms of IT certification is really popular. So I've started to talk to customers about the role of certification in their workplace. It turns out that

getting certified is important because it's tied to getting promoted."

This answer could be improved. How could you make it better? Let's break it down into **P-A-R** first.

"I use quantitative and qualitative approaches. Quantitative is looking at data to derive insights. Data can be what are customers doing when they use your product and, if you're working on a digital product, you could use an approach like web analytics. Qualitative approaches you can simply ask them about their needs about how they use your product, but a better way is to immerse yourself into their problem space and ask where does the product fit into their daily life today?"

This is the first part of the story, but it is not actually the **Problem/Situation**. It's what I call "general stuff" or "extra stuff we don't need." Many people add this type of info at the start of answers – but it isn't actually **"Problem"** stuff. It's not really giving you the situation.

How could you fix this?

Somewhat improved but still average answer:

P: I use both quantitative and qualitative methods to find out what my customers need. [I kept one sentence of the general stuff as a lead in – you could use more, but don't ramble on.] For example, last month I wanted to find out what type of content was most popular on our site so we could do more of it.

A: I looked at data on my top customers, in terms of the customers most engaged on my platform, and I could see that content about IT certification is very popular. So I started to talk to customers about the role of certification in their workplace. It turns out that getting certified is important because it's tied to getting promoted. As a result we started doing online trainings for the certifications. So instead of just a course or video, we do live trainings now as part of the educational product line up.

R: Those trainings turned out to be popular. So it seems that anything we give them in terms of IT certification is really popular.

I've eliminated the extra stuff in the first section that wasn't really related to the situation. You can see how applying the **P-A-R** technique and eliminating what didn't fit into that structure resulted in a much clearer answer.

Is this a great answer now? No, it's just average. You could improve this answer further by adding more details and/or data in each of the three sections. Although the first revision helped, the improved version was still a little light on concrete data. Any kind of details or numbers you have will make your answer sound more believable. The next version is even better.

Best version of answer:

P: I'm currently working at X, and our site is a learning platform primarily for enterprise customers. I use both quantitative and qualitative methods to find out what the customers want and need. For example, earlier this year, I wanted to find out what type of content was most popular on our site so we could do more of it.

A: I looked at data on my top customers, in terms of the customers most engaged on my platform, and I could see that content about IT certification was very popular. I wanted to dig deeper on this topic. I started to talk to customers about the role of certification in their workplace. It turns out that getting certified is important because it's tied to career growth, most specifically getting promoted. I also asked them what certifications they wanted the most.

Based on this research, we decided to increase our product offerings in this area. We already had courses and videos about certifications, but we added webinars to the educational product lineup because different formats appeal to a wider audience. To reach more users, we needed to diversify how the material was presented. We also increased the number and type of certifications we offered in areas where we saw the most interest – cloud-related technologies and security, for example.

R: Those trainings turned out to be popular. The average user now spends 23% more time per month on our learning platform, most of which can be attributed to our new IT certification-related materials.

Here's another example for that question given by someone from a different role.

Question: How do you figure out what a customer needs?

Answer given by a **UX Designer**:

"When I joined the team at X to work on their cloud product, I found out that there had been no customer research done prior to release of the first version of the product. It had been

primarily designed based on conversations with Sales Engineers. A quick usability tests proved my suspicions – customers found the product frustrating to use. One customer called the product a "chore to use"; another said it was "exhausting."

I met with the Customer Success Team to get a list of customers who had purchased this product. I then proposed a face-to-face user research meeting with them so I could understand these customers and get feedback on the version they were using. Before I visited, I created a test plan of questions I intended to ask and circulated it to the working team so that I could include questions they intended to ask.

I visited four customers and interviewed seven end users who were the primary users of this product. My selection criteria were as follows:

- Users who were using the cloud product currently (5)

- Users who had used it before and are no longer using it (5)

What I learned from my research was that there were two distinct personas who were intended to use it, the Manager persona and the Executive persona. The Manager wanted to have a much more detailed view into their subscriber activity and the Executive wanted to get a very high-level view. Apart from personas, I also learned that there were three focus areas of how the marketing teams worked (acquisition, upsell, and retention).

I synthesized this research and created a customer needs matrix, which acted as a key input to the product management prioritization roadmap. Our NPS score improved by 20 points as a result of this work."

This story is good because it uses a clear structure and has a story that answers the question. He is professional, straightforward, and direct. He weaves into his story phrases that make him sound like a subject matter expert – "usability tests," "user research meeting," "test plan," "end users," and "personas." He shows that he knows how to apply his craft to taking care of customers – "Customer Obsession."

Question: How do you show customer obsession?

A **Senior Digital Marketer's** answer:

"An example of how I regard customers is from when I had just become the Regional Manager at X bank in India in 2015. We were having problems retaining customers because our online services, in particular the online banking app, weren't as sophisticated as our in-person services were even though more of our customers were wanting to bank online. I realized this couldn't continue and began a push to revamp the app along with the IT department. It took us a year of product development but in the end we rolled out the new online banking app and service plan and it was well received. This and effort from other departments helped the organization notch customer engagement of 75 percent from 55 percent earlier over the next two years. We improved the region's profitability by 15 percent."

This is a good answer because he describes a specific problem and how he solved it. He also includes the results, which demonstrate that his solution was good for both the customer and the business.

The Action section is light on details though, which is a problem many candidates struggle with when forming stories. This story would be better if he had said what the problems were with the online app specifically and what was included in the new app that hadn't been there before and why those features were chosen. The Action section is the part of the story where you show how you made a difference. When you come up with your own stories, make sure you put in enough details.

I like the data that this candidate includes in his Results section. It's good if you can add data to your answers, both technical data and/or financial data. The data helps your answer sound like it was a real situation and also makes it sound like you have a high level of expertise. In other words, using data makes you sound smarter and more competent than if you don't talk about data, so it's good to have data in any answer.

Question: Tell me about a time where you put the customer first, regardless of what peers or management directed. What was the outcome? How did this impact day-to-day interaction with your peers and/or management?

Answer given by a **Cloud Architect**:

P: I worked with a mid-market client at X Co., when they were just making the transition to Azure cloud. Initially, they were just interested in lifting and shifting one of their web apps to the cloud for testing and development. They had paid less than $10K, making it a relatively small account.

Management didn't want me spending too much time getting them onboarded, but it was a relatively complex job and I wanted it done right.

A: I understood management's concerns, but I had done the architectural assessment and knew the client needs. My primary concern was doing right by the customer, but if I'm being completely honest, I saw significant upside opportunities. For one, while we had been contracted to migrate just the one web app to the cloud, the client in fact had a whole suite of apps that could eventually be migrated, if the first migration went well. Secondly, the client was well connected and would provide a reference for other work.

To convince management that this job was worth more time than usual for such a small account, I walked them through the hidden upsides. Since I had been working closely with the client I asked if I could spend time on this project until after go-live. My manager agreed, and I spent more time working on the project.

R: As a result of my close work with the client, the lift and shift was finished ahead of schedule. I wrote a proposal for the client to work on the other apps, which we ended up moving ahead with, and ultimately, the total contract value of the account surpassed six figures. That job influenced how we operated going forward, and fundamentally changed the role of Solution Architect at my company. The job was no longer just about meeting the exact requirements of the contract. We began engaging with customer needs more holistically, always seeking to deepen the relationship.

This a good story. The Solutions Architect shows that he can turn "Customer Obsession" into revenue opportunities. He also demonstrates that he's willing to fight for his ideas, which speaks to one of the other leadership principles ("Have Backbone").

Ownership

The second Amazon leadership principle is "Ownership."

Here's how Amazon explains the principle:

Leaders are owners. They think long term and don't sacrifice long-term value for short-term results. They act on behalf of the entire company, beyond just their own team. They never say "that's not my job."

If you're not clear on what this definition of "Ownership" means exactly, here are some other ways of understanding it. If you show ownership, you will:

- Ignore boundaries between jobs and departments if necessary to get your project done. If you see a problem and it's not in your department, you'll try to fix it.

- Along the same lines, you'll manage every dependency and won't make excuses if something goes wrong. You won't say, "That wasn't my job to take care of."

- Think about the impact of your decisions on other teams, sites, and the customer over time.

- Consider future outcomes (scalable, long-term value, and so on).

- Coach your team to understand the big picture, how their role supports the overall objectives of Amazon, and how it ties to others.

- Be willing to stretch outside the box / wear many different hats. For instance, you may have to perform sales activities even though you are in a marketing job.

Your interviewer may ask you to demonstrate your ownership skills. In the following section, let's review the top five questions related to "Ownership," based on my experience with clients.

Top five Amazon interview questions related to "Ownership"

1. Provide an example of when you personally demonstrated ownership.

2. Tell me about a time you went above and beyond. What actions did you take? Why did you take those actions? What was the outcome?

3. Tell me about a time when you took on something significant outside your area of responsibility. Why was it important? What was the outcome?

4. Describe a project or idea (not necessarily your own) that was implemented primarily because of your efforts. What was your role? What was the outcome?

5. Give an example of when you saw a peer struggling and decided to step in and help. What was the situation and what actions did you take? What was the outcome?

Question: Provide an example of when you personally demonstrated ownership.

Here's a **Senior Product Marketing Manager**'s answer:

"When I was leading the Marketing Services team, we were told to have digital media investments as twenty percent of the product's fixed marketing expenses in two years. At the time, the digital share was only five percent of expenses, with display and banner ads and some YouTube videos.

The business teams were the key responsible people for budget management and allocation. My role was to give them direction on the most effective way to spend based on the communication strategy. Both marketing teams and the media agencies were hesitant to make such a big shift in a short period because the ROI wasn't known. My task was to convince the business leaders to invest more on digital campaigns.

I led four major initiatives. First, I collaborated with digital platform owners on Facebook, Twitter, and Google to give training on digital and social media to the marketers and build key campaigns together and used their data combining with brand metrics to evaluate performance. Then I started reverse mentoring in the company. Younger team members showed us how they were interacting with brands and what they liked doing in social media. This increased our organizational competency for digital. I also asked our creative and media agencies to include more digital talent. Last, I restructured the marketing KPIs and brand health tracking to incorporate the evaluation of digital campaigns. This enabled us to learn what drives ROI.

At the end of the second year, more than twenty percent of the budget was being invested in digital. One campaign won the Facebook Cannes award and the other won the Twitter Aviator award."

This story follows the PAR structure, demonstrates ownership, is about the right length, and is easy to follow. For those reasons, it's a good story. How could we make it even better? I think this story would be stronger if it had better focus. The candidate telling the story says that her task is to convince business leaders to invest more. When I read this story, it sounds like she was successful in convincing them when she "restructured the marketing KPIs and brand health tracking" to "learn what drives ROI." However, she provides little detail on that topic and instead talks about other initiatives that were not directly connected to persuading the business leaders. My advice in this case would be to **focus more on the main problem** (convincing business leaders) and how the candidate solved it (demonstrating ROI).

Let's look at another example.

Question 2. Tell me about a time you went "above and beyond." What actions did you take? Why did you take those actions? What was the outcome?

Here's one **Software Developer**'s answer:

"While working on my most recent project, our customer asked to add a new feature to the product. While it was a reasonable request, it went beyond the scope of the project we had worked out, and there was no time built into the schedule for it. My manager decided that we couldn't

refuse and insisted that we rework the schedule. This change increased my workload about 25% in the same timeframe. I did my best to complete the extra work in the time given by working later at night and also working some of the weekends. Although it wasn't an ideal situation, we managed to pull it off and the customer was satisfied with our work."

The story needs more details. This developer should add details about the company she was working for, the type of product, the feature, and the work she was doing to make for a stronger answer. Why did the manager insist on doing the work? Who was the customer? Details help make the story sound more real.

Also, "above and beyond" means doing more than what is required, so in other words if you do something extra it will be something that isn't already in your job description. Weren't the things she's talking about here just her normal everyday job? How are they outside her normal work? I don't think they are, so this wouldn't be a good choice to answer this question. See the next question/answer for a good answer to the "above and beyond" question.

She could use this answer for doing something quickly or helping a customer.

Question 3. Tell me about a time when you took on something significant outside your area of responsibility. Why was it important? What was the outcome?

This is an **Operation Manager**'s answer:

"As a part of a company rebranding, we were moving our site to a new domain. The old domain had gained significant domain authority over the years and, at the time, was generating trials worth $4.50 each, and we were getting approximately 1,000 per day. The goal was to complete the migration while protecting that line of revenue.

I didn't see anyone treating this project with the sense of urgency or risk mitigation that I thought it needed, so I took over coordinating it, although it would have normally fallen to the marketing team to lead this effort. While I wasn't an expert, I had researched best practices around a site migration. I was convinced that the key was to migrate the content pages, set up 301 redirects, and have Google re-index the site as quickly as possible. It was inevitable that we'd lose some revenue during the migration, but I knew we could minimize it with decisive action and SEO best practices.

I led the team through the implementation, while carefully monitoring the organic traffic data during the migration. We completed the migration as planned. While we initially saw a decline in organic traffic (as expected), it recovered quickly. We had successfully migrated to the new domain and still met our B2C budget numbers."

This is a solid answer. The Operations Manager saw an opportunity to help with an important company initiative and showed leadership by taking on a project that was outside of his department.

This is a similar question to the "above and beyond" one, but this is something that is clearly outside of this person's normal area of work and so it answers the question better than the Developer did.

Question 4. Describe a project or idea (not necessarily your own) that was implemented primarily because of your efforts. What was your role? What was the outcome?

Digital Marketing Manager's answer:

"Last year we weren't getting high enough conversion rates on some of our pages for our newest product. They were well below our goal. I was managing the team whose goal was to fix this. I coordinated our landing page optimization efforts and we updated the user interface on 10+ landing pages in less than three months. We saw conversion lifts between 25 and 45 percent."

The structure of the answer is solid, but it's missing details and so is **too short**. This person could add explanation for what the products were, what the pages that weren't converting were, and more details about how she fixed the problem.

What skills should a person in this role have? Add details that show you have those skills when expanding your story.

Better version:

"I'm a Digital Marketing Manager at X, a company that sells X. Last year we weren't getting high enough conversion rates on some of our pages for our newest product, the XX. The pages for X, Y, and Z had conversion rates that were well below our goal and what was considered best in class conversion rates according to industry norms. My personal goal was to achieve conversion rates that exceeded those norms.

I was managing the team whose goal was to fix this issue. I coordinated our landing page optimization efforts, and we updated the user interface on 10+ landing pages in less than three months. In updating the pages, we focused on creating much clearer calls to action. We also rewrote all of the copy and positioning to make it much more about the value that the product provides versus just a feature list. While we were confident in our product, our user research revealed that users were more likely to convert if we focused on the benefits that the product provides. In other words, we tied the conversion event directly to consumers improving their lives.

While we did have to iterate over a few versions to get it right, we kept at it. With each update, we ran a fresh set of user tests to gauge our progress. This approach was successful, and we saw conversion lifts between 25 and 45 percent, which met the goals that I had set for myself and my team. This increased conversion would ultimately lead to a 25 percent increase in sales month over month."

Question 5. Give an example of when you saw a peer struggling and decided to step in and help. What was the situation and what actions did you take? What was the outcome?

Senior Business Development Manager's answer:

"At my current job, a recent product launch opened up an opportunity to enter into the financial sector, a new market for us. I had come from this world and knew it intimately. In truth, I was the best qualified person to plan how we would penetrate the market, but I was deep into closing a major deal and didn't have the bandwidth. My colleague

stepped up and was preparing a plan. When he asked for my advice, I saw that he was missing some of the key players in the space and would struggle to penetrate the market.

It wasn't as simple as me telling him who he needed to talk to. To be successful, he needed to approach it in a specific way. The incumbents are very entrenched in the financial sector, and it's more about the relationships than the products themselves. It was a lot to talk through. I asked him if he was free for dinner, and we worked together on his plan through dinner and well into the evening. I laid out for him who specifically he needed to approach, and how to manage the relationships. I also mentored him on having patience as these deals would take time to develop but would be worth it in the end.

He closed his first deal with a bank in Germany five months later, which would lead to a string of opportunities. We expanded the team, and the financial sector became a major line of business for us."

This story needs more data, but it's a compelling story and the BizDev Manager shows maturity and leadership in his answer. To improve this answer, the BizDev Manager should attach a financial metric to the "string of opportunities" that he refers to in the Results section of the story. That addition would change it from a good story to a *great* one.

Invent and Simplify

The third Amazon leadership principle is "Invent and Simplify."

Here's how Amazon explains the Invent and Simplify principle:

Leaders expect and require innovation and invention from their teams and always find ways to simplify. They are externally aware, look for new ideas from everywhere, and are not limited by "not invented here." As we do new things, we accept that we may be misunderstood for long periods of time.

The "invent" part of this principle is that Amazon frequently does new things, whether "new" means new scale, new products, new platforms, or something else new.

The "simplify" part of this principle is the idea that everyone, no matter what type of job they have, has the opportunity to simplify something, usually a process. Making something simpler is desirable because simpler usually equals greater efficiency, i.e., quicker or cheaper, and what company wouldn't like that?

Amazonians are always thinking about how to make things smoother, faster, cheaper, and better for the customer. Oftentimes this takes the form of "kaizen" or continuous process improvement and automation.

My clients sometimes worry that, if they're not inventing new products or new technologies as part of their job, they won't be able to answer questions about the Invent and Simplify principle. But that's not true. You don't have to be "inventing" things to do well on this principle. Anyone in any type of role can have an impact on a process.

So besides wanting to know if you've invented or simplified, what is your interviewer looking for when she asks you to speak to this principle? Amazon wants people who are curious and well informed and can be creative in thinking of solutions. They want people who can easily generate multiple ideas for problem solving. They want people who know how to find answers by looking into how other departments or other industries do things. Above all, they want people who will try to improve things, not just accept the status quo blindly.

Top five Amazon interview questions asking about "Invent and Simplify"

There are different questions your interviewer can use to ask about your "invent and simplify" skills. Based on my experience with clients, here are five common questions:

- Tell me about a time you invented something.

- What improvements have you made at your current company?

- Tell me about a time when you gave a simple solution to a complex problem.

- Tell me about a time you had to think outside the box (think creatively) to close a sale or sell your product.

- What is the most innovative project you've worked on?

Question: "What improvements have you made at your current company?"

Answer given by a **Data Engineer**:

"We were using an Enterprise Service Bus in our project for SOA, and one of the functions we use it for is to record the time when a web service request arrives at our platform and when the response leaves the platform. Logging this information helps us measure response-time performance analysis for each web service. The response-time data were stored in a database which has grown very big as the platform has expanded over the years.

We needed to keep the growth of the database in check. Per project requirements, it was also necessary to keep data available for three months online and one year in an offline storage.

I developed a tool that met and automated the requirements. Once the user configures the tool, it automatically finds the table partitions in scope, backs up those partitions, zips up the backup, and then moves the backup to tapes. As the final step, it generates SQL script files to clean up the partitions that it had backed up.

As a result of this automation, we saved at least one to two days of effort per month. We are also using this tool to clean up the logs for provisioning history from customer records."

Stories related to automation are well suited for "Invent and Simplify" questions. Note how this Data Engineer includes the results of his work – "two days of effort per month." In your own stories related to "Invent and Simplify," follow this example and include specific business outcomes.

Question: "Tell me about a time you had to think outside the box."

The phrase "outside the box" means "not the usual way of looking at things." If your interviewer asks you this question, you need to provide evidence that you question assumptions.

Answer from a **Product Manager**:

"We had a SAAS product [note: SAAS is "software as a service"] that needed to integrate with our clients' human resources platforms. We had two target markets – healthcare and academic. Both markets offered large opportunities, but, to me, the TAM [note: TAM is "total addressable market"] of the healthcare customers was much more attractive.

The problem was that healthcare customers tended to use one type of HR platform, and academic customers used all sorts of different types. The technical team struggled with an integration solution that would work in all situations. It became apparent that we would need to build several disparate solutions, not one as we had hoped, to service both markets.

The business owner of our unit was dismissive of these technical hurdles, but I spent time with the teams, and I knew this complexity was going to add months and even threaten the feasibility of the project. I ran the numbers and put together a presentation, demonstrating to the business owner and several senior stakeholders that we should focus on the healthcare market and revisit the academic market in the following years. I had to do a lot of convincing because, as I said, the academic opportunity was large.

Eventually I convinced the business that we needed to simplify our approach and focus on the larger market and build a solution that would work for those customers."

Note how this interviewee questions assumptions, digs into the details, and is willing to stand up for the best solution for the business, even when his seniors thought otherwise. The solution presented wasn't a small improvement to the existing business model; it was an entirely new idea for the company and one that wasn't conventional wisdom of trying to make all customers happy so you don't lose any of them.

Let's look at one more example for the "Invent and Simplify" principle.

Question: Tell me about a time you invented something.

Answer given by a **Senior Software Engineer**:

"Three days before a big release, my customer identified that the infrastructure testing had not been completed. They would not go ahead with the release without completing testing. Specifically, the customer wanted to test the firewall connectivity between servers, and they wanted to check if the health checks were all green on the load balancers. All APIs were already responding as expected.

I stayed at the office late that night and logged into each box and ran a set of telnet commands to complete the tests. It was simple but repetitive work. After doing this for about a quarter of the 100 servers, I had had enough and knew I had to automate the process. If I continued working in the same way, I'd never finish in time, and my approach was prone to human error.

Unfortunately, due to company policy, the client hadn't granted me the level of access I needed to create script files on the servers and execute them. So I explored a method using Java-based shell API Jcraft JSch. I wrote the proof of concept in my own workspace, completed it on the same night, and sent the results to my client contact. He was impressed and thought the approach looked sound. Based on that exchange, I built my POC into a tool that was used by the entire team.

With the tool in place, productivity improved, and we were able to complete the testing in time for the release."

In the story, the Senior Software Engineer was under tremendous time constraints, and she had limited access to the server to automate in the way she normally would. When you are trying to think of stories for "Invent and Simplify," think back to the times in your career when you were under constraints but still got the job done. To "Invent and Simplify," you must do something in a new way, either new to you or new to your business. Try to capture that spirit of "newness" in your own "Invent and Simplify" stories.

Are Right, A Lot

I usually get questions from my interview coaching clients about what this principle means because it's a hard one to understand.

Here's how Amazon describes this principle:

Leaders are right a lot. They have strong judgment and good instincts. They seek diverse perspectives and work to disconfirm their beliefs.

Here's an excerpt of *The Amazon Way* by John Rossman, a book you should read if you want to know more about Amazon. Rossman explains the thinking behind this principle better than I can. This should help you understand what the principle means:

"Leaders at Amazon are right—not always, but a lot. They have strong business judgment, and they spread that strong judgment to others through the clarity with which they define their goals and the metrics they use to measure success.

There is a high degree of tolerance for failure at Amazon. But Jeff Bezos cannot tolerate someone making the same mistake over and over. Therefore, leaders at Amazon are expected to be right far more often than they are wrong. And when they are wrong—which of course will happen when a company continually pushes the envelope—they are expected to learn from their mistakes, develop specific insights into the reasons for those mistakes, and share those insights with the rest of the company."

That should have helped a little, but I know the principle still isn't that easy to understand. If you keep reading the meaning will become clearer.

I think of the principle as being about judgement, but "judgement" is a big concept. Because it's such a big concept, it's hard to pin down. How do you know if someone has good judgement? There are many behaviors someone might display that show their judgement or lack of judgement. Because there are so many layers to the judgement idea and so many behaviors one might display that show judgement, there is no one single typical question for this principle.

Let's look at some ways in which an interviewer might ask about this principle. The first way is what I call "the mistake or failure questions."

The mistake or failure questions

These are popular questions. The interviewer might use different words to ask this question, such as "failure" or "mistake" or "error in judgement" or "bad decision" or "regret." You can use the same example for your answer no matter how the question is asked. Yes, you can use the same answer for the regret question too, just make sure you explain why you feel regret (what did you do wrong that you now regret?).

How to answer?

1. First, admit you made a mistake.

   Try to avoid talking about messing up something that's business critical. If the job you're trying to get is manager of X and, in your example, you talk about how you did a bad job with X yesterday, consider another approach. Try a topic that doesn't cast doubt on your skills, or pick an example from early in your career so you can show how you learned to do X better afterward. Ideally, you want to choose a story that talks about a skill more removed from your potential duties at Amazon. Or you want to pick an example from early in your career so you can show how different you are now because you've learned.

2. Quantify your mistake, if possible.

   Talk about how much revenue was lost or how much time was lost due to your error. What effects did your mistake cause?

3. Talk about what you learned from your mistake.

   The "learning" part of the answer is necessary.

4. Link your learnings to a recent success.

   You learned something from your mistake and then you applied this new improved knowledge to your future projects. Give an example of where you had a successful outcome as a result of your new knowledge.

A good failure story needs to show a negative impact on others. If you did something wrong in your previous position but there were no consequences, then it's probably not a big enough mistake. A good example is if you lost a client and your team suffered or if you failed to meet a deadline and a project is canceled.

How not to answer mistake or failure questions:

Don't be overly hard on yourself. Yes, admit you made a mistake. But don't talk about how you can't believe you did this and you're so sorry and you know how stupid it was, etc. Everyone makes mistakes and it's necessary to be calm and straightforward when talking about them.

Don't say you've never made a mistake. This shows that you're dishonest or don't realize when you make mistakes. Dishonesty and lack of self-awareness are ways you fail this question.

Don't say that your biggest failure is something very small like that you forgot to turn in your benefits forms, etc. This is a common thing that people do when they're not used to being open about their failures. And don't do the reverse psychology tactic where you say, "My biggest failure is that I work too hard." If you have an experienced interviewer they will be secretly rolling their eyes at you for this.

Sample answers to mistake or failure questions
Question: Tell me about a time you failed.

Answer given by a **Big Data Consultant**:

"I worked for a company's big data practice as a senior big data consultant for enterprise. One of our clients, X Communications, the second largest U.S. cable operator, wanted to build two hundred nodes using Hortonworks Hadoop clusters. This was an important client for us. I worked with the client's big data manager on an analysis and determined the level of effort to be sixty days with four Hadoop admin resources to complete the build.

Unfortunately, I missed the project deadline because I failed to manage the scope creep. The project extended an extra sixty days. It cost us one extra month of billing four Hadoop admin resources worth a hundred thousand dollars.

During the project, the business requirements changed repeatedly, requiring support for HBASE, Kafka, Sqoop, and

Ranger, which significantly increased the overall scope of the project. I flagged this scope creep in our weekly status meetings, came up with updated level of effort estimation of another sixty days, and presented it. I also created an updated project plan and explained the deviation from the original sixty days to the client's big data manager. I offered the option of including the new requirements in a subsequent project, but I couldn't persuade him.

From this failure, I learned that I need to be more vocal and have a stronger backbone. Going forward, I committed myself to engaging with the client manager and stakeholders in brainstorming sessions at the requirements phase to avoid scope creep. Also, I learned I should propose agile methodology/scrum framework for implementing this kind of project, even when the client was unfamiliar or even resistant.

Soon after, I managed a similar project with another client. When the client was vague on requirements, I told them about my experience with the Charter project and what it had cost us. Because of my experience and approach, the new client listened to me and decided to go with the agile model, which helped us to tightly manage the scope. We were able to deliver that project on time and we generated five hundred thousand dollars in revenue, largely because we managed scope and delivered on time."

Notice how specific he is in talking about what he learned. The best part of his answer is how he emphasizes how he turned his experience from a past failure to future success. This might be a risky choice of topic to use because dealing with scope creep is essential in this person's job. Ideally you should choose an answer that shows a significant mistake or failure but not one so terrible that you sound incompetent.

Answer given by a **Senior Technical Account Manager**:

"This was when I was on my Company X project. One of the applications was generating a lot of temporary files and was not cleaning it up. We had logged a bug with the application team. However, in the meantime, I had taken up a task to clean up the files hourly. I developed the script quickly as it was simple. Got it peer reviewed and put it in PROD. Everything was working fine. The following weekend we had a code deployment. We implemented a new tool for deployment. The deployment completed and we released the application for testing.

After some time, we got complaints that the testing team was seeing errors and no one was able to get to the application. I tried myself and I was not. Upon checking I found out that the ear file I deployed was missing. I knew I had deployed it and checked before releasing. So, I could not understand what happened. I checked with my coworkers and no one had done anything. So, I quickly redeployed, checked, and released for testing. I also kept working in the background to find the root cause. In some time, the issue resurfaced and I saw the same behavior. The files were missing. Then I realized maybe some process is removing the files. Also, I noticed a pattern that the complaints came at the top of the hour. So, it struck me that it may be from my script. I checked the script logs and found out that it was the case. I quickly removed the script. Then upon analysis I found that the new tool that we had used had created a symlink in the path of the application. This caused the find command to fail and the xargs that was piped to it and running rm picked up the wrong files and created them.

I conveyed this to my manager. I also gave him all of the technical details. I fixed the script and manually tested it a few times and put it back. This was very embarrassing for me as I had wasted two hours of downtime.

The mistake I made was not to have a check for when the find command fails. I did not build error handling on that. So, this incident made a large impact on my future scripts. Now I make my scripts donkey proof at each step. It adds a few lines in the code and some extra executions, but I'd rather be safe than sorry."

Her answer is good because she does admit the mistake and say how she learned from it, but it would be better if she mentioned the mistake earlier. She doesn't get to it until the last paragraph, so the earlier part of the story is full of technical details with not much space given to analyzing her behavior and mistake. You need to spend at least a few sentences talking about what you did wrong and what you learned from it.

The interpersonal conflict questions
How you act in the middle of a conflict is a good indicator of how you relate to people.

These questions are often similar or identical to the ones you'll get asked in the Have Backbone questions.

How to answer?

Show you're (1) a nice person but (2) you can be firm if your opinions are challenged and know how to be firm enough to achieve your goal. A good answer will show both (1) and (2). Unfortunately, a lot of people focus only on (2), so they show how they met their goal but also show that they were difficult to work with. I think most people don't realize they're showing the interviewer that they're difficult to work with or have difficulty with interpersonal relationships.

Do interpersonal relationships really matter? Well, Amazon fosters a culture of assertiveness (some call it "sharp elbows"). In a culture like this it can be hard to meet your goals while also maintaining good relationships, but if you destroy your relationships you will probably ultimately not be able to achieve your goals because your goals often involve working with other people. This is really the reason you need to show you can "get along with" others, because someone who can't will ultimately not be successful at Amazon because no one will want to help them.

A good way to show that you're nice is to show that you can be calm and have rational discussions if you're challenged. Talk about how you had a discussion with the person you disagreed with.

Besides showing you're nice, you also have to show that you're capable of achieving your goal. If you have an opinion on something but someone doesn't agree, do you agree with them to end the conflict? Or do you discuss the issue until you can convince them you're right (if you are)? Show that you can use data to prove that your opinion is the right one. Showing data about your side of the argument is the perfect way to "win" the conflict in a respectful way.

Sample answer for the interpersonal conflict question

Question: Tell me about a time you disagreed with a colleague (or a boss). What is the process you used to work it out?

Answer given by a **Director of Software Development:**

"I recently had a disagreement with my team about whether a specific functionality should be rolled out in production. The early testing we did showed a potential negative impact on website performance that could result in a drop in user engagement and usage of a $5B USD product. Emotions were high and the opinions were strong.

The first thing that I did was to draw a line of sight for my team about how this functionality was critical to the long-term strategy of the company and the potential upside if we got it right. Then I agreed with my team about key business metrics that we would monitor in production. This included full text access and FTAs/session. If we didn't see a meaningful impact then we would know that the new functionality is safe and would not impact our business negatively.

We agreed to roll this out in an A/B test fashion first to 5% of the traffic and then slowly ramping up to 50%. We would run this for a few weeks and go to 100% when we'd achieved statistical significance. At any given time if we saw a problem we could ramp down to 0%.

I got an agreement from my team on this approach, and everyone was reasonably happy to try out this way. We are currently at 75% and hopeful that we will be 100% within 2 weeks."

This answer is **average**. The conflict is with a team, not one person, so it doesn't convey any actual conflict or "drama." She says "Emotions were high" but that is a vague statement, not a description of the disagreement. What were some specifics of the disagreement?

A better story would be one that is with one person and then she would talk about what that person thought and said and what she said in response. She would talk about how she showed the other person data in order to convince them that her idea was better. I know you normally wouldn't talk about those kind of small details – what you each said – but in these conflict questions you should do that.

Better version:

"I recently had a disagreement with the Lead Developer on my team about whether a specific functionality should be rolled out in production. The early testing we did showed a potential negative impact on website performance that could result in a drop in user engagement and usage of a $5B USD product. He thought it was too risky and we shouldn't do it but I thought it was worth the risk.

I sat down with him and discussed the issue. The first thing I did was to explain how this functionality was critical to the long-term strategy of the company and the potential upside if we got it right. I explained that even though it was a risk it would be worth it if it worked. Then I agreed with him about key business metrics we would monitor in production. This included full text access and FTAs/session. If we didn't see a meaningful impact we would know that the new functionality was safe and would not impact our business negatively.

We agreed to roll this out in an A/B test fashion first to 5% of the traffic and then slowly ramping up to 50%. We would run this for a few weeks and go to 100% when we'd achieved statistical significance. At any given time if we saw a problem we could ramp down to 0%.

The two of us agreed and then convinced the team on this approach, and everyone was happy to try it this way. We are currently at 75% and hopeful that we will be 100% within 2 weeks."

The judgement or data questions

These are questions asking about how you make decisions (how do you collect data you can use to decide something, do you have good judgement, etc.).

So how to answer?

Just describe what process you used. Be specific. Did you throw darts at the wall to choose what to do? Probably not. What did you do instead? How do you usually solve problems or make decisions? This isn't a trick question.

Don't skim over the actual research process. Say where you got information, even if you think this information is too basic or boring. Don't just say that you "got the information from the database." What information? What database?

They want to know if you have good intuition, and how you put that intuition to work. Intuition is partly using your past experience to make decisions. You can talk about that past experience and how it informed this decision.

They also want to know how you make decisions. What is your general process? Talk about that.

Sample answer for the judgment or data questions

Question: Give me an example of when you had to make an important decision in the absence of good data. What was the situation and how did you arrive at your decision? Did the decision turn out to be the correct one? Why or why not?

Answer given by a **Consultant**:

"I was working in the Private Equity Group at X. The practice conducts commercial due diligence for private equity, which means that we pressure test the target company's market growth, competitive dynamics, and profit upset before the firm acquires it. The due diligence timeline is usually short, between 1-8 weeks. I worked on a project investigating a trustee services provider in AU and NZ. I had about 3 days to form a recommendation on whether the NZ market represented a major opportunity for this target.

Based on my past experience, this question translated into 4 points of data needs. I typically go through a consistent approach to data gathering. After step 1 of the data gathering, I already knew there were significant data gaps in the securitization segment as well as the market share data for the managed funds segments.

The securitization segment was only $30B. It would not change the final answer. I was happy to make a business decision to not pursue it further. But I needed to figure out the market share piece so I called the experts regarding market share of the managed funds segment. I also gathered reports on the largest funds in NZ and went through their product disclosure statements. I also arranged expert calls with the largest funds to understand whether their choice is likely to change in the future.

Based on the outcome of my research, we formed the view that the NZ market was not exciting. The client was very pleased with our work as it answered their most strategic questions and presented data they had never seen before."

This person could have added **more details** to make the answer a little more specific. For instance, what are all types of data needs? What is the typical approach to data gathering? What is more background on why she was doing those steps?

To know how many more details to add, you can time your answer. If it's already 3 minutes long, you may have enough details. But if it's under 3, think about more you can add to get it at least 3 minutes. You don't want to go over 4 minutes because that can be too boring, but you want it to be at least 3.

Other possible interview questions for Are Right, A Lot

- Describe a situation where you thought you were right, but your peers or supervisor didn't agree with you. How did you convince them you were right? How did you react? What was the outcome?

- Tell me about a time you strongly disagreed with your manager on something you deemed to be very important to the business. What was it about and how did you handle it?

- Tell me about a time where someone openly challenged you. How did you handle this feedback?

- Give me an example of when you took an unpopular stance in a meeting with peers and/or your leader and you were the outlier. What was it, why did you feel strongly about it, and what did you do?

- When do you decide to go along with the group decision even if you disagree? Give me an example of a time you chose to acquiesce to the group even when you disagreed. Would you make the same decision now?

- Tell me about a decision for which data and analysis weren't enough to provide the right course and you had to rely on your judgment and instincts. Give me two to three examples.

- Tell me about a time you made a difficult decision and how you knew it was the right solution (how you evaluated the options, if you received input, what data you reviewed, etc.)

- Give me an example of when you had to make an important decision in the absence of good data because there wasn't any. What was the situation and how did you arrive at your decision? Did the decision turn out to be the correct one? Why or why not?

- Tell me about a time you had to fix something but had no data or direction.

- Tell me about a time when you were faced with a challenge where the best way forward or strategy to adopt was not "clear cut" (i.e., there were several possible solutions). How did you decide the best way forward?

Learn and Be Curious

The fifth Amazon leadership principle is "Learn and Be Curious."

Let's look at how Amazon explains the principle:

Leaders are never done learning and always seek to improve themselves. They are curious about new possibilities and act to explore them.

This is an easy principle to understand. It's asking you if you are the kind of person who is always learning and improving. How do you keep up with the trends and new developments in your field? Do you try to do things a new way even if there's no "need" for it? Are you open to learning new things?

They want to know you're curious because curiosity leads to creativity, which leads to new ideas and innovation.

What are some typical interview questions that require you to address the "Learn and Be Curious" principle:

- How do you find the time to stay inspired, acquire new knowledge, or innovate in your work?

- How do you keep up with best practices?

- How do you keep up with industry trends and what your competitors are doing?

- What have you learned that has helped you in your job?

- What is the coolest thing you've learned on your own that has helped you better perform your job?

- Tell me about a time you learned something new from your peer or your direct report at work.

- Tell me about a time when you solved a problem through just superior knowledge or observation.

- Tell me about a time when you influenced a change by only asking questions.

- What is a recent book you've read and what did you learn from it?

- Tell me about a project that required you to learn something new.

- Tell me about a time you took on work outside of your comfort area and found it rewarding.

- Tell me about a time you found you needed a deeper level of subject matter expertise to do your job well.

- Tell me about a time you didn't know what to do next or how to solve a challenging problem.

- Give me an example of a time when you challenged the notion that that something had to be done a certain way because it had always been done that way.

- What are you working on to improve your overall effectiveness at work?

- When we enter a new role or problem space, it is common to come in and see things with a fresh perspective. Tell me about a time when you realized that you might have lost that fresh perspective. What ended up happening?

- What is an example of how you've connected the dots to come up with a counterintuitive solution?

- Tell me about a time you hired someone smarter than you. (Manager)

- Tell me about a time when you challenged your team to push the envelope and go beyond existing standards and expectations. (Manager)

- Give me an example of a time when someone on your team challenged you to think differently about a problem. (Manager)

Format for answering "Learn and Be Curious" questions
Do you need to answer these questions the same way you answer other behavioral questions – in the P/A/R format? No. Some of these questions are the exception to that rule. For some, instead of P/A/R, you can just give a list of what you do, like you'll see in the following examples. Or you can give a general statement first, like "I love to learn new things and for my job I always have to keep up with the new developments in X" and then after that give the list of what you do.

Sample answer for "Learn and Be Curious"
Question: How do you stay inspired, acquire new knowledge, or innovate in your work?

Answer given by a **Director of Product**:

"For my job I need to understand business trends, so I read several newspapers every day, including the Wall Street Journal, the New York Times, and the Washington Post. I also read magazines, including the Economist and the New

Yorker. *In addition, I spend quite a bit of time reading news on Twitter and other places online. As a Product Director for an EdTech company, I oversee a team that produces videos, books, and courses on tech subjects, so I also absorb a lot of the newest information while I'm reviewing our products and our competitors' products."*

This answer is good, because it demonstrates that the interviewee prioritizes learning in his daily habits, which he ties directly back to what is useful for his job. Ultimately, the interview is about knowing whether you can do the job, so your answers should relate to the job duties. If you don't need to know what is happening in politics or economics for your job (many people don't) you wouldn't say that you read newspapers, for example.

Answer this question by being honest about how you keep up with new technology and new trends in your field. What do you do? You probably read blogs, newspapers, and/or books, or maybe you listen to podcasts or watch YouTube videos. There are probably other things you do too – do you take classes at a local school or online, somewhere like Coursera or EdX? Are you enrolled in a certification program? Did you just finish a degree? I've also had clients successfully answer questions about this principle by describing a lecture series that they attended at lunch in their offices or a conference where they met industry leaders.

Show your interest or passion when you talk about whatever it is you do.

Don't tell the interviewer you don't have the time to do any of these things because you have a family and a job. I hear this answer a lot from clients, and I warn them that it's a mistake. The interviewer will think you're a bad candidate if you don't have a list of ways you're keeping up with new developments.

I know that we're all busy and it's hard to do your job all day and then learn more in your free time. But the people you're competing with for the job you want are definitely spending their free time taking classes or going to conferences or reading, even though their lives are just as busy as yours.

Another example by a Solutions Architect:

"I always try to stay up to date with the latest technology. I go to conferences and meetups relevant to my work and interests and read books and follow all major technical publications. I stay current with my credentials and certifications. I recently passed my AWS Solutions Architect exam and am now preparing for the second set of exams. I follow ThoughtWorks Technology Radar and I have recently learned a lot about Micro-Frontends, and we are now building a framework to allow all teams to build FE applications that way."

Notice how this candidate begins by answering the question generally, but then gives examples, before ending her answer with a very specific skill that she learned and recently applied to her work. Formatting your answer in a similar way is a good strategy.

Question: What have you learned that has helped you in your job?

Answer given by a **Senior Technical Account Manager:**

"My job has made me research a lot of new technologies, so I have learned a lot about Oracle's Fusion Middleware platform. I have also done quite a few automation tasks. That gave me an understanding of CI/CD and made me appreciate the ease and agility with which you could complete your SDLC now compared to a few years ago."

Answer given by a **Technical Account Manager**:

"I started my career as an Oracle System DBA and worked for Oracle as a consultant. I began to see Application DBAs as a very interesting area. Because Application DBA is responsible for everything (DB, web server, form server, reporting server, and so on). I discussed this with my boss, and he sent me to an Apps DBA training class. Very quickly I was on the projects where I was working in an apps DBA role. I began to learn even more and did more implementations. I wanted to learn more and transferred to work with one large development org in Oracle to work as Apps DBA. After working with Oracle development, I went back to Oracle consulting and worked on exciting implementation projects for my consulting org's customers."

While both of these answers are fine, the second answer is stronger because the candidate takes the time to explain the impact of what he learned in specific detail.

Hire and Develop the Best

The sixth Amazon Leadership Principle is "Hire and Develop the Best." Let's look at how Amazon explains the principle:

Leaders raise the performance bar with every hire and promotion. They recognize exceptional talent, and willingly *move them throughout the organization. Leaders develop leaders and take seriously their role in coaching others.*

What does the "Hire and Develop the Best" leadership principle mean?

They want to know your management style and how you have developed people in the past. Can you hire the right people, ones who can do the job exceptionally well but who're also interested in growing, and then help them learn and succeed in their job and their overall career?

Who will get asked about this principle?
This is a principle you won't get asked about if you're not a manager. If you are a manager, you should prepare an answer that will work for each category of these questions – hiring, managing performance, building a team, etc. You can't just have one example for the entire principle, because there are so many different activities under "managing" and the stories aren't interchangeable.

Do candidates for IC roles need to prepare for this principle?

This principle is targeted toward candidates for roles that manage other people, not for roles that are individual contributors (ICs). If you are applying for an IC role, you don't need to worry about this one, except for the "coaching a junior employee" or "giving feedback to another employee" or the other questions about coaching someone who isn't your direct report.

Other principles for people manager roles
Hire and Develop (#6) and Strive to be the Earth's Best Employer (#15) are the two principles for people managers.

If your interviewer asks about this leadership principle, he or she might ask one of the following questions:

- What is your management style?

- How do you approach managing your reports?

- What is your experience with hiring people?

- How do you ensure you hire the best people?

- Give me an example of one of the best hires of your career. How did this person grow throughout their career? What did you identify during the hiring process that drove her success?

- How do you help your employees grow?

- Tell me how you helped your team members develop their careers. Can you give me two to three examples of a specific person in whom you invested and how you helped them develop their careers, including one who wasn't being successful but in whom you saw potential and chose to invest?

- Give me an example of a time you provided feedback to develop and leverage the strengths of someone on your team. Were you able to positively impact that person's performance? What were your most effective methods?

- How do you manage your top performers differently?

- Give me an example of someone who was promoted one or two levels up in the organization, not just because they were a star who would naturally rise, but due to your coaching efforts.

- What is the composition of your current team, and how is your team organized?

- How have you been successful at empowering either a person or a group to accomplish a task?

- Tell me about a time when you were able to remove a serious roadblock preventing your team from making progress.

How to answer questions related to this principle

You'll want to demonstrate certain skills as you answer these questions.

- **You know how to hire excellent people.**

  You take the interviewing process seriously. You understand the job and identify the right job description and candidate profile to attract the best candidates. You focus on hiring people who will raise the high performance bar.

- **You recognize strong performers and mentor them.**

  At some companies, good performers are left alone – because they are already doing a good job – and bad performers get all the attention – to improve their performance. Amazon is what is called a "high-performance management culture," which means that the company believes that top performers need attention and guidance to ensure that they have the opportunity to provide their best at Amazon.

  If you currently work at a company where the attention goes to low performers, you should reorient yourself before you think of your answers to this. Since Amazon believes that spending time on top performers is one of the best uses of a leader's time, don't say that you spend an equal amount of time mentoring your employees, whether they're top performers or not.

- **You try to help your people grow. You make it a priority to coach and teach employees. You provide regular feedback.**

  Of course you want to keep the best performers on your team, because you want good workers, but as a leader and manager, you need to care about their careers as well as your team performance. If you can help an employee learn, they will at least be likely to stay with the company as they grow, even if not on your team.

  Show that you know what each employee wants and that you are trying to help them achieve that goal. You help employees drive their own development and learning by regularly discussing career goals, strengths, and areas for development. Show that you identify development activities and moves for all employees.

- **Diversity is a strength and will help you stand out.**

  Do you hire people you feel comfortable with or do you hire the best person for the job?

  Tech has a diversity problem, and if you are a white man (which many of my clients are), you are probably not very aware of diversity. If you've created a team that isn't all white men, consider it an accomplishment and be prepared to speak to it.

How did you make diversity a priority? This is a strength you can talk about.

Question: What is your experience with hiring people?

Answer by a **VP of Sales**:

"When I took over the sales team, the CEO told me that my number one priority needed to be hiring. We didn't have enough people to meet our goals for the year. Focusing on hiring was hard for me because I knew there were a lot of processes that we needed to work on as a team besides hiring, but I agreed to focus my efforts there because I knew that the best thing I could do in the long term for the team was to make it more resilient.

It was true that most members of the team had been around for a while and we really needed some new faces help execute against the new strategy. My approach first and foremost was to tap into my own network, which is pretty deep, and seek out the people who were the best I had ever worked with. I specifically went after people who I was a little intimated by because of their deep skills, because I knew it wasn't about me but about making the team stronger. The second thing I did was to tap into my team's network. I told a key number of them that hiring needed to be one of our top priorities, and we came up with a process for screening and interviewing candidates. This approach worked and became self-perpetuating because, as new people came on board, and became excited about what we were doing as a company they recruited from their own network."

This answer is good because it shows that this VP understands the idea of hiring excellent people, in particular how to focus on hiring people who will raise the performance bar. She doesn't let her ego get in the way of hiring smart people, maybe people who are even smarter than she is.

You can probably use a version of this answer yourself, no matter what job you're in, because this is a common situation, although of course you'll need to customize it to your own experience.

Question: Tell me about the best hire of your career.

"The best hire I ever had was also my toughest hire. I knew the candidate for Product Manager was strong, but she continued to hold out and ask a lot of questions. She wanted to talk to other members of the team, and she wanted to know everything about the company. The process went on for so long I started to question whether it was worth it. I was pretty frustrated and wasn't sure what I was going to do, but a colleague gave me some great advice, convincing me that the candidate who asks the best questions usually turns out to be the best person for the job. I decided to remain patient with her and when she (finally) came aboard, she hit the ground running and soon became one of the star performers in the company. She's actually managing the department for me now. I learned a lot about what talent really looks like from the experience."

This answer emphasizes the quality of the person being hired. He was willing to wait and put up with aggravation to get someone excellent. It could be improved by giving more details about what job he had or what kind of company it was.

Question: Give me an example of a time you provided feedback to develop and leverage the strengths of someone on your team. Were you able to positively impact that person's performance? What were your most effective methods?

"As I got to be a more senior manager and started hiring managers, I was hiring people who were further into their career. I started to see that they didn't need as much guidance as I had been used to giving. I realized that what they really needed was someone to help them clear the path so that they could succeed. I changed the way I dealt with those type of employees; now I make it a priority to meet with them one-on-one and let them set the agenda. I tell them that at our meeting we will have nothing to talk about unless they bring something to talk about. They tend to bring things up that are blocking them. We talk about that and either I intervene directly or I give them advice on how to clear the roadblocks.

On the other hand, if that someone is on the wrong path, I let them know right away. In the past, I would sometimes give my team the benefit of the doubt and not share my feedback. I learned that not helping them see what I see was really a disservice to them. Now I give feedback early and often, and if someone is on the wrong path, I help them see it. Feedback is ongoing and built into the culture of the team, not something that happens quarterly."

This answer is good because he's focused on developing his strong performers, rather than spending his time on the weak ones. Note how he emphasizes that he's learned from his past experience and how he's capitalizing on that experience for the good of his team and the company. This is the type of person that Amazon wants to hire for a senior manager-type role.

Insist on the Highest Standards

The seventh Amazon Leadership Principle is "Insist on the Highest Standards." If you're preparing for an interview at Amazon, you should ask yourself what Amazon means by "highest standards" and how this principle applies to your role at the company.

Let's look at how Amazon explains the "Insist on the Highest Standards" principle:

Leaders have relentlessly high standards – many people may think these standards are unreasonably high. Leaders are continually raising the bar and driving their teams to deliver high-quality products, services and processes. Leaders ensure that defects do not get sent down the line and that problems are fixed so they stay fixed.

What does this principle mean?

Having high standards means you make exceptionally high demands of yourself and the products and services you work on. At Amazon, standards are set through service level agreements (SLAs). An SLA is a set of agreed upon standards at which any service or product will perform. In an Amazon SLA, even the worst outcome will outpace industry standards.

Nearly everything at Amazon has an SLA, and as such, nearly everything is measured to ensure the SLA standards are met. In your current job, have you taken the time to instrument your processes and services? Have you set clear expectations of success that you can measure via that instrumentation? If so, in your interview, be ready to tell your story.

If you want to show your interviewer that you insist on the highest standards, you should demonstrate that you:

- Set SLAs for everything, and don't take shortcuts on instrumentation.

- Continually self-critique your work to make sure the quality is the best it can be.

- Accept and seek coaching and feedback from your manager and others about improving the quality of your work.

- Demand that your team delivers high-quality products, services, and solutions.

- Coach employees about setting their own high standards and exceeding customer expectations.

Interview questions related to this principle
If your interviewer asks about this leadership principle, she or he might ask one of the following questions:

- Tell me about a time when you've been unsatisfied with the status quo. What did you do to change it? Were you successful?

- Tell me about a time you wouldn't compromise on achieving a great outcome when others felt something was already good enough. What was the situation?

- What measures have you personally put in place to ensure performance improvement targets and standards are achieved?

- Describe the most significant, continuous improvement project that you've led. What was the catalyst for this change and how did you go about it?

- Give me an example of a goal you've had where you wish you had done better. What was the goal and how could you have improved on it?

- Tell me about a time when you worked to improve the quality of a product / service / solution that was already getting good customer feedback? Why did you think it needed more improvement?

- Give an example where you refused to compromise your standards around quality/customer service, etc. Why did you feel so strongly about the situation? What were the consequences? The result?

How to answer questions related to this principle

Question: Tell me about a time when you worked to improve the quality of a product / service / solution that was already getting good customer feedback? Why did you think it needed more improvement?

Answer given by an **E-commerce Manager**:

"When I took over the ecommerce part of the website, I learned that the experience related to returning merchandise was one of the worst experiences on the site. It

was difficult to navigate, and when I asked why it was so bad, the answer I got from senior management alarmed me. They didn't want the experience to be easy because they didn't want people to return things. This felt intuitively wrong to me, but I knew I needed the numbers to prove it. I began collecting data relating to return customers and how the return had an impact on how likely they were to return. After a lot of digging, we learned that if a customer had a good return experience, they were more likely to buy from us in the future. We set off to create the most frictionless return experience possible and then we measured the impact of the customer to return and what they were likely to purchase. As we made changes to the return experience, we carefully measured the impact."

Note that, in this answer, the candidate could have simply followed along with the established protocol, but he sought to hold himself and his company to higher standard, demonstrating real leadership and delivering results.

He did say "we" a lot in his answer, which isn't a good idea. You want to talk about what you yourself did, not what your team did, unless you're leading a team.

He could have added **more details** – What was this company selling? Why was the return process difficult specifically? How did you collect the data on the process? What did they "dig" into?

Question: What measures have you personally put in place to ensure performance improvement targets and standards are achieved?

Answer given by a **Solutions Architect**:

"In my last job, when I joined the solutions architect team, my main goal was to ensure that our enterprise clients integrated seamlessly with the solutions we were providing. I became obsessed with the onboarding of these customers and one metric in particular, which was the time the client signed the contract to the time they first used the services. To me this was the metric that mattered the most, but we weren't paying much attention to it. I knew that if we showed the value that our service provided sooner, they would be more likely to stay with us over the long term. We measured and then optimized processes based on what we found. For a good while in that role, nearly every measurement of success I created for myself and my team rolled up onto the larger onboarding metric. As a result of these efforts, over the course of a year, and ruthlessly optimizing our processes, we cut the average time of onboarding down by 50 percent."

She could have added **more details**. What company was this? Why solutions did they sell? Why weren't they paying attention to that metric? Why does showing value early keep clients long term? What processes did they optimize?

As in the previous answer, this candidate demonstrates that she absolutely will not settle for the status quo, and so she sets a higher standard for her and her team. Leaders don't need someone else to set the bar high, because they set it high for themselves.

She also said "we" a lot, and so she should try to balance that with saying "I."

The eighth Amazon Leadership Principle is "Think Big." If you're preparing for an interview at Amazon, you should ask yourself what Amazon means by "think big" and how this principle applies to your role at the company.

Let's look at how Amazon explains the "Think Big" principle:

Thinking small is a self-fulfilling prophecy. Leaders create and communicate a bold direction that inspires results. They think differently and look around corners for ways to serve customers.

What does the "Think Big" principle mean?

The term "to think big" means to be ambitious or to set no limits on your thinking and goals. Other expressions you might have heard that mean the same thing are "to go large" or "to reach for the stars."

If you "Think Big" you will:

- See problems as challenges and opportunities
- Be positive
- Think of things you can do, not things you can't
- Plan what is possible, not worry about what is impossible
- Be fearless
- Be creative
- Be able to dream and visualize what you want

Thinking big means:

- Taking a radical approach and risks when necessary, always questioning traditional assumptions in pursuit of the best idea.

- Creating a gutsy mission that employees can be inspired by and get behind. Providing direction for how to get there and explaining how everything fits into the long-term plan.

- Continually communicating the big picture and mission to the team in a manner that gets employees excited.

- Actively exploring new ideas from team members, encouraging risk taking when appropriate.

Interview questions related to "Think Big"

If your interviewer asks about this leadership principle, she or he might ask one of the following questions:

- Tell me about a time you took a calculated risk to achieve a professional goal. What were the tradeoffs? What was the outcome?

- Tell me about a time you took a big risk and it failed. What did you learn? What would you do differently?

- Tell me about a time you went way beyond the scope of the project and delivered.

- Tell me about your proudest professional achievement.

- Give me an example of a radical approach to a problem you proposed. What was the problem and why did you feel it required a completely different way of thinking about it? Was your approach successful?

- How do you drive adoption for your vision/ideas? How do you know how well your idea has been adopted by other teams or partners? Give a specific example highlighting one of your ideas.

- Tell me about time you were working on an initiative or goal and saw an opportunity to do something much bigger than the initial focus.

- Tell me about a time you looked at a key process that was working well and questioned whether it was still the right one. What assumptions were you questioning and why? Did you end up making a change to the process?

How to answer questions related to "Think Big"

Question: Give an example of a time you took a calculated risk.

Answer given by a **Data Architect**, who specializes in building and maintaining disaster recovery systems:

"On a yearly basis, Huawei works together with its customers to perform the disaster recovery drills. In this drill, we switch over all our services from one data center to another in a controlled fashion. A few months ago, while we were preparing for the drill, we met an issue that could have blocked the whole activity. A colleague was performing a regular check on hardware resources when we found that the number of CPUs on a database machine disaster recovery site was not matching the number of CPUs on the production site.

He requested a change window, brought the machine down, changed the number of CPUs to match the production site, but then the machine was not able to startup. After a few calls with KVM experts at HQ, we understood that the HQ experts couldn't find the root cause and the solution was to rebuild the disaster recovery machine. To our surprise, we weren't able to reuse resources allocated to that dead virtual machine to a new virtual machine. Fortunately, we had another environment hosted in VMware, and we had resources available to host a new machine. I suggested that we host the failed disaster recovery database in this new platform, which was considered risky because none of the other disaster recovery machines were running in VMware.

The customer was worried that hosting the failed machine in the VMware environment would mean a machine on production and the disaster recovery databases would be hosted in a different hypervisor environment. Their apprehension was understandable, since no customer/vendor would host machines in such a way. However, I explained to them that Oracle is agnostic about which hypervisor it is running on. As long as the OS version, OS type, and DB version are the same, Oracle would work without a problem.

Therefore, going against the normal way of doing things, I rebuilt the 6.5TB database in a VMware environment in 20 hours. A day later we successfully performed disaster recovery switchover and switchback operation."

This candidate used his technical expertise for "thinking big," i.e., a willingness to solve a problem in an unconventional way. His confidence in his own expertise mitigated what others would have perceived as a "risky" technical maneuver.

Question: **Give an example of how you set goals**.

Answer given by a **VP of Digital Product Development** at large financial institution:

"I tend to set very ambitious goals for my team and also myself professionally. An example of this is that, as soon as I joined my current company, I knew I wanted to lead an organization. I set small goals to achieve that ultimate goal.

I needed to be the best individual contributor on my team, and I did that by delivering the Merrill Lynch mobile application platform for financial analysts. I was recognized for this and was promoted within a year and a half of joining. I then set my sights on the next milestone, which was to lead multiple teams and manage multiple apps on multiple platforms. This is when I hired someone really strong to delegate some of the mobile platform work under me, so that I could oversee the creation of the desktop platform for financial analysts.

I led the design and implementation of the Client 360 app, which was our internal flagship app. The work required that I coordinate across seven different teams, each one building components in isolation before eventually integrating them into one single-page app.

I was recognized for my leadership quality during this effort and was promoted again in two years. Since that time, I have managed to deliver multiple applications, such as

Client Profile and Relationship Tree on the desktop platform, while continuing to grow the mobile app customer base.

I am the youngest of all my peers, and they all had a VP title before me. But because of my hard work, dedication, and relentless pursuit of perfection, I am being considered for my next promotion this year before all my peers."

This is a more personal topic than the first answer, but this is fine because the question was more personal because it asked about a personal behavior and not a past experience. I think you should avoid using examples that talk about your personality or personal life rather than job-related experiences for most of the interview but it's fine if you want to use one or two.

The candidate's ambition really shines through in this answer. Note how she "thinks big" and tackles the most ambitious projects but is always looking ahead to the next challenge.

Bias for Action

The ninth Amazon leadership principle is "Bias for Action." If you're preparing for an interview at Amazon, you should ask yourself what Amazon means by "Bias for Action" and how this principle applies to your past experience and to your future role at the company.

Let's look at how Amazon explains the "Bias for Action" principle:

Speed matters in business. Many decisions and actions are reversible and do not need extensive study. We value calculated risk taking.

What does the "Bias for Action" principle mean?

Having a bias for action means you're not afraid to make decisions and take action, even when (especially when) you face uncertainty. Maybe you've worked with someone or a team who didn't have a bias for action. In the face of uncertainty, these individuals freeze and can't make a decision. They're afraid of getting it wrong and being held accountable for making a poor decision.

This sort of "analysis paralysis" isn't tolerated at Amazon. They want leaders who are willing to put themselves out there and take a risk. These leaders are no different than anyone else in their fear of failure. What makes them stand out is that they accept risk and make calculated decisions that unblock them and the people they work with. Yes, Amazon wants you to look at data and make sense of it and use it to form your plan, but they don't want you to get stuck looking at the data. They want you to move past research and analysis into action.

Here are the characteristics of someone having a "Bias for Action":

- When faced with a tough decision that will help you and your team move forward, you don't avoid that decision. You're not afraid to step up and make the call.

- You encourage this same behavior in your direct reports. You let them know you'll stand behind them if they take a risk that doesn't work out.

- If you're missing some key piece of information, you try to get it as quickly as possible. If you can't, you're not afraid to move ahead without it.

- You foster an environment of action bias by responding promptly to colleagues looking for information, and always deliver on your promises.

- You roll up your sleeves and remove obstacles, even when it's "not your job."

- Still stuck? You ask for help. You don't let yourself or your team be stuck for days at a time.

Interview questions related to "Bias for Action"
If your interviewer asks about this leadership principle, she or he might ask one of the following questions:

- Tell me about a time you took a risk. What kind of risk was it?

- Give me an example of a calculated risk that you have taken where speed was critical. What was the situation and how did you handle it? What steps did you take to mitigate the risk? What was the outcome?

- Tell me about a time you had to make a decision with incomplete information. How did you make it and what was the outcome?

- Describe a time you had to make an important decision on the spot to close a sale.

- Describe a situation where you made an important business decision without consulting your manager. What was the situation and how did it turn out?

- Tell me about a time you had to analyze facts quickly, define key issues, and respond immediately to a situation. What was the outcome?

- Tell me about a time you worked against tight deadlines and didn't have time to consider all options before making a decision. How much time did you have? What approach did you take?

- Give an example of when you had to make an important decision and had to decide between moving forward or gathering more information. What did you do? What information is necessary for you to have before acting?

- Describe a time when you saw a problem and took the initiative to correct it rather than waiting for someone else to do it.

- Tell me about a time you needed to get information from someone who wasn't very responsive. What did you do?

- Tell me about a time you felt your team was not moving to action quickly enough. What did you do? (Manager)

- Tell me about a time you were able to remove a serious roadblock/barrier preventing your team from making progress? How were you able to remove the barrier? What was the outcome? (Manager)

How to answer questions related to "Bias for Action"

Question: Tell me about a time you had to make a decision quickly.

Answer given by a **Senior Backup Engineer**:

"We had to expand the storage capacity of a Commvault server to accommodate new machines that were coming

online. We planned to double the capacity of the server from 32 to 64 terabytes. For this upgrade, the server had to be converted to MediaAgent, a procedure that was documented and tested. We followed the documentation closely, but in production, the Windows batch file that was supposed to convert the server to MediaAgent accidentally deleted some important files on the server, effectively rendering the existing Commvault server useless. All backups from applications/DB started failing.

While experts from Commvault HQ were engaged to find the root cause, the customer was informed about this problem. In an hour, I determined that the problem was not easily fixable. I wanted to use a new server, but the Commvault license was linked to a particular IP address. Instead of waiting to hear back from Commvault HQ and our purchasing department on getting another license, I simply copied the XML license to a new machine, changed the IP, and updated the existing license. At that point, the team could move forward."

How does this answer show a "Bias for Action"? With the backup server rendered inoperable, the engineer in this story was faced with a big problem. The more time she wasted, the more backup data would be lost. But she didn't wait for others to solve her problem. She quickly diagnosed the problem and identified a workaround that would get the team back on its feet. That's a "Bias for Action."

Question: Tell me about a time you had to make a decision quickly.

Answer given by a **Solutions Architect**:

"One of the largest insurance providers in North America has been a long-standing customer. They had been using a different vendor's solution for UNIX bridging capability. Once they learned that we also offer a UNIX bridging solution, they wanted to conduct a proof of concept. As I had been working with that customer as a trusted advisor, they requested me to do the POC.

Before starting the POC, I had a working session with the customer's technical team to review the use cases currently being implemented. Upon reviewing the use cases, I found out that one of their key use cases is not supported out of the box by our solution. Supporting that use case would require an enhancement to the existing product functionality. Given the importance of the POC, I reached out internally for an approval to engage the engineering team immediately and worked with the team in adding that capability to the product. I didn't want to wait to do this.

The engineering team provided a patch in a short time, and I was able to successfully deliver the POC addressing all the use cases."

In this story, the Solutions Architect could have told the customer that the product doesn't support the use case. Instead, he coordinated with his team a quick product update (a "patch") that would accommodate the use case, leading to a successful POC. This answer shows a "Bias for Action" and true "Customer Obsession"!

Frugality

The tenth Amazon Leadership Principle is "Frugality." If you're preparing for an interview at Amazon, you should ask yourself what Amazon means by frugality and how this principle applies to your past roles and your future role at the company.

Let's look at how Amazon explains the "Frugality" principle:

Accomplish more with less. Constraints breed resourcefulness, self-sufficiency and invention. There are no extra points for growing headcount, budget size or fixed expense.

What does the "Frugality" principle mean?

If you're frugal, you try to save money. You'll want to show you can do the job without spending more and that having not enough time or resources is fine. Resource constraints are not a huge problem that will stop you from succeeding; it's something you can deal with.

However, you can be "frugal" with more things than money. You can also save time or other resources, including person hours.

It's not that Amazon is cheap. In fact, the "Frugality" principle is not necessarily about saving money at all. The logic behind this principle is that Amazon uses frugality as a forcing function – meaning that the company believes that constraints can help drive creativity and innovation. After all, if you don't have money to spend, you'll have to find ways to do things more cheaply or efficiently.

Interview questions related to "Frugality"
If your interviewer asks about this leadership principle, she or he might ask one of the following questions:

- Tell me about a time you thought of a new way to save money for the company.

- Describe a time you had to manage a budget (or manage time/money/resources/etc.). Were you able to get more out of less?

- Tell me about a time when you had to work with limited time or resources.

How to answer questions related to "Frugality"

Question: Tell me about a time when you had to work with limited time or resources.

Answer given by a **Category Marketing Manager**:

> *Note* This person managed a mileage program at a major gas company.

"After I presented the scope of our new rewards program to my supervisors, they approved the strategy. However, we did not have the budget to afford all of the components of it. Therefore, I would have to modify my plan. I began to explore other ideas.

At this point, I had a partnership contract with a Brazilian company for the prizes of our giveaways. I decided to try and negotiate with them a sponsorship for the first year of the program by showing that my business plan was forecasting an increase in traffic to their marketplace, which would result in many new customers and sales. Besides that, I could communicate their program to millions of people in our gas stations and in our app.

Fortunately, they ended up sponsoring the first year of the program, and I was able to launch it in that same quarter. This program turned out to be very good for the partnership because 70 percent of our customers were redeeming their points for miles (not discounts), which was the goal of the project. Additionally, every month, we sent thousands of new customers to Smiles' Marketplace, as was forecast in the business plan. My plan increased the number of transactions on their website from 100,000 to 330,00 per month."

In this answer, the Marketing Manager describes how she found a creative way to resource against an approved strategy by leveraging an existing partnership. Note in her answer that she accepts but is undeterred by the business constrains of a limited budget. Her resourcefulness and creative problem-solving skills demonstrate a "Frugality" mindset.

Question: Tell me about a time where you thought of a new way to save money for the company.

Answer given by a **DevOps Engineer**:

"My company wanted to speed up and have improved monitoring for software deployments to our production environment. The management team was convinced that we should use a third-party tool, and we started to explore options. I attended a number of demos with the team, and we all agreed on the best third-party tool. I thought that the tool was good, but it was costly, and even though it was a management decision, I couldn't shake the feeling that we should explore the option of building the tooling in-house for long-term cost savings.

I analyzed the level of effort it would take me and the team to build the same core functionality of the third-party tools, and I included maintenance cost over time. I compared that cost to the cost of the third-party license and added the additional cost that we would incur integrating these third-party tools into our systems. I presented my findings to the management team. Based on my analysis, we changed course, and saved significant costs, especially over the long-term."

In this answer, the DevOps Engineer demonstrates a "Frugality" mindset around a decision that wasn't even his to make. The easier way forward for the engineer would have been to just go along with the plan and be done with it, but leaders know that waste hurts the team and the company. If you have a "Frugality" mindset, the financial health of the company is always factored into your decision making.

Earn Trust

The eleventh Amazon Leadership Principle is "Earn Trust." If you're preparing for an interview at Amazon, you should ask yourself what Amazon means by "Earn Trust" and how this principle applies to your role at the company.

Let's look at how Amazon explains the "Earn Trust" principle:

Leaders listen attentively, speak candidly, and treat others respectfully. They are vocally self-critical, even when doing so is awkward or embarrassing. They benchmark themselves and their teams against the best.

Let's take a closer look at this principle.

The first sentence of the principle is straightforward and expected in any professional environment. The interview is a great opportunity for you to "Earn Trust" by listening to your interviewer attentively and answering questions candidly.

In the second sentence of the "Earn Trust" principle, things get more interesting. At Amazon, you are expected to win over your colleagues (i.e., earn their trust) by being "vocally self-critical." In other words, you're not afraid to point out your own faults to others. To win trust, you must show that you understand best-in-class standards, and that you seek to meet or exceed them.

So how do you "Earn Trust"? Leaders at Amazon embody this principle by:

- Consistently making good decisions
- Keeping commitments
- Treating others and their ideas with respect
- Adhering to high ethical standards
- Admitting failures
- Listening, communicating, and delegating to help employees get the right things done

Leaders "Earn Trust" when they "take the hit." When undesirable outcomes happen, we're all quick to point the finger. If your team members see that you're willing to take the blame for the good of the team, even if it's not directly your fault, then they'll start to trust you. As leader of a team, you need to accept the responsibility for both the good and the bad.

True collaboration is only possible in an atmosphere of trust. And that atmosphere must be set by a leader who has earned his team members' trust and who trusts them in return.

If your interviewer asks about this leadership principle, she or he might ask one of the following questions:

- Tell me about a time you had to earn trust quickly.

- Building trust can be difficult to achieve at times. Tell me about how you've effectively built trusting working relationships with others on your team.

- Describe a time when you significantly contributed to improving morale and productivity on your team. What were the underlying problems and their causes? How did you prevent them from negatively impacting the team in the future?

- Give an example of a time you were not able to meet a commitment to a team member. What was the commitment and what prevented you from meeting it? What was the outcome and what did you learn from it?

- Describe a time when you needed the cooperation of a peer or peers who were resistant to what you were trying to do. What did you do? What was the outcome?

- Tell me about a piece of direct feedback you recently gave to a colleague. How did he or she respond?

- How do you like to receive feedback from coworkers or managers?

- Tell me about a time when someone (peer, teammate, supervisor) criticized you about a piece of work/analysis that you delivered. How did you react? What was the outcome?

- Tell me about a time when you had to tell someone a harsh truth.

- Tell me about a time you had to communicate a big change in direction for which you anticipated people would have a lot of concerns. How did you handle questions and/or resistance? Were you able to get people comfortable with the change?

- How do you convince someone who is resistant to what you're trying to do?

How to answer questions related to "Earn Trust"

Question: How did you quickly earn your client's trust?

Answer given by a **Solutions Architect**:

"One of the largest mass entertainment companies in North America purchased licenses for product X and signed a statement of work (SOW) for Professional Services for implementing the solution.

I was the architect and hands on technical resource for doing the migration. I created detailed standard operating procedures, end user training materials, and delivered end user trainings once the solution went live in production, even though these weren't in the scope of the services SOW.

I was engaged in building the long-term deployment roadmap, working very closely with customer's stakeholders. By demonstrating strong technical acumen and client-facing skills, I was able to earn trust in a short period of time. I quickly became part of the customer's inner circle.

The solution was successfully deployed, and we went live with one of their key services in production. The initial SOW was for a three-month engagement, but we stayed with the customer for about two years delivering services. We were able to successfully expand the solution capabilities during that period, assisting the customer in further enhancing their security protocols."

In this story, notice how the Solutions Architect credits her "technical acumen and client-facing skills" for winning the customer over. But earlier in the story, she described how she had already demonstrated that she was willing to go above and beyond the requirements of the SOW to make the project successful. In other words, she set a higher standard for both herself and the project. This type of behavior will help you "Earn Trust" at Amazon.

Let's look at another answer for the same question, this time from an **Account Executive**:

"One of the large full-service banks in North America had already purchased our product licenses to manage the company system permissions and user identity. Due to organizational changes, the new leadership team had decided to shop for alternative solutions, and compare/contrast all the functional/technical capabilities before finalizing a single solution. My accounts team brought

me in to talk about the solution, and why it would be a good fit for this client.

As a first step, I flew to L.A. and conducted an all-day workshop with the key stakeholders to carefully listen to their concerns and reasons for the vendor solution review exercise, as well as to understand their business and the technical requirements. We had good discussions during this workshop. I told them that I agreed to some of the areas of improvements in our product and made a note of them for an internal product management team review. At the same time, I was candid in my feedback regarding some of the requirements and suggested alternative options to minimize operational overhead in the long run.

By the end of the day, the client wanted me to work with them in conducting a proof of concept (POC) in their environment. I believe listening attentively to the customer, speaking candidly and demonstrating sound technical and communication skills helped me in gaining trust in a short period of time. I was able to deliver the POC successfully and in turn signed a professional services SOW contract of about eight hundred thousand dollars."

After reading this story, return to the section above and read the "Earn Trust" principle again. I hope you can see that the story demonstrates the principle almost perfectly. Note in the story the emphasis on attentive listening. Note also how the person telling the story is willing to admit that the product has faults. It's easy to see why this person won the customer's trust.

Question: Tell me about a time you coached someone and provided feedback

Answer given by an **Engineering Manager**:

"One of the senior managers complained about one of the developers on my team regarding his tone being too harsh and frank in his emails and over the phone. My manager brought it to my attention, and I told him I would take care of it.

I immediately pulled this employee in for a one-on-one and brought this to his attention. I told him it was not what he said but how he said it that makes all the difference. There are more politically correct ways to provide feedback to other teams regarding their mistakes.

He agreed that he reacted out of frustration and promised me he would be more careful going forward. It has been a year now, and he has completely turned it around. He had numerous accolades from other managers regarding his integrity, and he is now one of the rising stars on my team."

This story highlights a theme I see again and again in working with professionals across all walks of life. As hesitant as we sometimes are to give feedback, when we set aside our fears and give honest, candid feedback, people are often extremely appreciative and grow because of it. This story demonstrates another way to "Earn Trust." It can also work for coaching under "Hire and Develop."

Dive Deep

The twelfth Amazon Leadership Principle is "Dive Deep." If you're preparing for an interview at Amazon, you should ask yourself what Amazon means by dive deep and how this principle applies to your role at the company.

Let's look at how Amazon explains the "Dive Deep" principle:

Leaders operate at all levels, stay connected to the details, audit frequently, and are skeptical when metrics and anecdote differ. No task is beneath them.

What does this principle mean?

I think of this principle as being on a continuum with the "Bias for Action" principle. When you're doing something, it doesn't matter what, you first need to figure out what you're doing (research and think) and then you need to do it (act). I find it helpful to think about these two principles as a continuum because job seekers tend to get stuck on one end of it. It's not uncommon for candidates to be great at performing research but slow to act, or on the other end of the continuum candidates will jump into action too quickly without making a plan first.

To be good at something – it doesn't really matter what – you need to be good at both making a plan and acting on it. So in an interview, you want to be able to answer the "Dive Deep" questions and also the "Bias for Action" questions well, so that you paint a picture of yourself as someone who can make a plan and act on it. A good "Bias" story will have a research phase and a good "Dive Deep" story will end in action.

A good "Dive Deep" should preferably include data borne of research. Telling "Dive Deep" stories like this might be easy for you if you're a details person, as many people who have technical jobs are. It may not be easy for you if you're a generalist or a big picture person. I personally tend to dislike talking about details, because I prefer talking about ideas or strategy. If I were going into an interview, I would need to add details about how I followed through on ideas. If you're a big picture person, pay particular attention to your "Dive Deep" stories. On the other hand, if you're someone who routinely digs into details, these questions are unlikely to be difficult for you because you're always looking at data and you may actually have to cut your stories so they don't run over four minutes.

Ex-Amazon employee and blogger Dave Anderson <u>summarizes the principle this way</u>:

"Trust yet verify" is a favorite phrase at Amazon. We care deeply that leaders keep a careful eye on what they own, and know ways to audit their space. If something doesn't make sense, our leaders need to have the ability (and interest) to dive in and figure out what's going on.

I love when I ask questions of people, and they can go four or five levels deep, and keep getting more excited because the details are actually interesting to them.

Note the emphasis here on not just digging into the details, but getting excited about those details when you talk about them. If you're asked to speak to this principle in your interview, it's not enough to list details – you need to use those details to demonstrate your enthusiasm for owning or contributing to a project.

Interview questions related to "Dive Deep"
If your interviewer asks about this leadership principle, she or he might ask one of the following questions:

- Give me an example of when you used data to make a decision/solve a problem.

- Tell me a time you gave insights beyond the data.

- Have you ever leveraged data to develop strategy?

- Tell me about a time you were trying to understand a problem on your team and had to go down several layers to figure it out. Who did you talk with and what info proved most valuable? How did you use that info to help solve the problem?

- Tell me about a problem you had to solve that required in-depth thought and analysis. How did you know you were focusing on the right things?

- Walk me through a big problem in your organization that you helped solve. How did you become aware of it? What info did you gather, what was missing, and how did you fill the gaps? Did you do a post mortem analysis and what did you learn?

- Can you tell me about a specific metric you've used to identify a need for change in your department? Did you create the metric or was it readily available? How did this and other info influence the change?

How to answer questions related to "Dive Deep"

Question: Tell me about a time you performed an analysis that resulted in process improvements.

Answer given by a **Systems Engineer**:

"The process for monthly mobile phone bill generation was slow. The bill generation process for one hundred and thirty thousand subscribers took twelve hours. I was asked to

analyze whether there were opportunities to optimize the process.

Unfortunately, we had minimal documentation available on the process. I held a session with the application support engineers to understand how we could trace this process. After that, during the next bill cycle, we traced all database calls for twelve hours. Then I consolidated over a thousand trace files in chronological order and ran an Oracle profiler called tkprof.

My analysis revealed that the process spent lots of database time in performing single block reads and multiblock reads. The total time spent in doing I/Os was six hours. Approximately half of disk I/Os were taking more time than normal. After a similar analysis in preproduction, I saw that, even with 25% more subscribers, the bill run finished in the same time as production. The difference was that the preproduction environment had a newer CPU and a newer storage system. Part of the performance improvement in preprod was also the result of less traffic going into the preproduction environment. I/O took a lot less time in preprod.

After this analysis, I presented the findings in a twenty-six page report and a brief presentation. My recommendations were as follows:

- *Move bill run data to a dedicated database*

- *Cache smaller tables in memory*

- *Move bill run data to faster disks*

As a result of my recommendations, we started the hardware modernization project, and as expected, newer CPUs and storage helped a lot. We were able to improve the performance of bill runs by approximately 35%. We brought down the bill run time from 18 to 12 hours. A big improvement, but I know I could make more progress."

There are a lot of details in this answer from the Systems Engineer but note how seamlessly he weaves technical details into his story about a business process improvement. Even more importantly, note how he turns research into action. He "dives deep" but uses the information to make concrete recommendations, showing a "bias for action."

Yes, the point is that you are great at doing research, but you still have to connect it to some action or your research was pointless. You don't have to do the action yourself, but you can't do the research and do nothing with it.

Question: Walk me through a big problem in your organization that you helped to solve. How did you become aware of it? What info did you gather, what was missing, and how did you fill the gaps?

Answer given by a **Data Scientist**:

"There are different kinds of spam; it relates to the season. For example, there is a different kind during Christmas, the Super Bowl, the Oscars, etc. Spammers use campaigns to insert some kind of scam in text messages.

During the political campaigns last year, I was working on an assignment to detect spam in politics-related text messages. There is nothing wrong with doing campaign by text message, although it can be annoying, but the intention was to detect malicious messages within the body of these messages.

I started to analyze the data by isolating messages related to politics and then, once I had a good sample of these messages, I used data science and machine learning techniques to identify different patterns that could be not related to certain campaigns. I started by defining a base of target words which I will look for in the body of the message, and then I clustered together the most common words surrounding this base sample. It took me a very deep dive in the data to find common words that are used in a masked way, for example, one word separated by periods, numbers substituting for some words, etc. I could only do this by analyzing a lot of data.

At the end of the research, I tuned my code to automatically perform the analysis and deliver reports or alerts whenever this kind of spam was detected. To improve my detection analysis, I continued adjusting and fine-tuning my code as new results and/or patterns were discovered."

This Data Scientist uses machine learning techniques to surface patterns to filter spam that would otherwise be difficult to catch. Note how diving deep into the data seems to come naturally to her, as she tells her story. To an interviewer at Amazon, you need to show that you're not afraid to get into the details when the situation calls for it. I find when working with clients whose jobs revolve around data they don't have a problem finding stories to talk about but they have a problem giving proper context for their story, structuring the stories clearly, and remembering to connect the data to some kind of result or action.

Have Backbone; Disagree and Commit

The thirteenth Amazon Leadership Principle is "Have Backbone; Disagree and Commit." If you're preparing for an interview at Amazon, you should ask yourself what the company means by having backbone and how this principle relates to the role you're applying for.

Let's look at how Amazon explains the "Have Backbone" principle:

Leaders are obligated to respectfully challenge decisions when they disagree, even when doing so is uncomfortable or exhausting. Leaders have conviction and are tenacious. They do not compromise for the sake of social cohesion. Once a decision is determined, they commit wholly.

What does this principle mean?

What does the phrase "to have backbone" mean? It's an English idiom that means to have strength, particularly in the face of adversity. If I "have backbone," it means I will stand up for my ideas.

- You should show that you fight for your ideas, not that you give up on them if someone challenges you.

- What if you fight for your idea (meaning you "disagree" with someone) and don't win - what do you do then? Do you support the person who did win ("commit" to their idea) or do you try to work against them because your idea didn't win? You need to show you will support them.

- You should also act like a mature adult. Don't yell, don't blame anyone else for any problems, and listen to the other person. You can also talk about what you learned from the difference of opinion.

If you haven't read my section on "Are Right, A Lot" you should read that, because that principle includes how you manage conflict, which is related to the "Have Backbone" principle. Both principles deal with interpersonal relationships, in particular conflicts that arise between two people (or one person and a group of people).

Interview questions related to "Have Backbone"
If your interviewer asks about this leadership principle, she or he might ask one of the following questions:

- Describe a situation where other members of your team didn't agree with your ideas. What did you do?

- Tell me about a situation where you had a conflict with someone on your team. What was it about? What did you do? How did they react? What was the outcome?

- Tell me about a time when you did not accept the status quo.

- Tell me about an unpopular decision of yours.

- Tell me about a time when you had to step up and disagree with a team member's approach.

- If your direct manager was instructing you to do something you disagreed with, how would you handle it?

- Describe a situation where you thought you were right, but your peers or supervisor did not agree with you. How did you convince them that you were right? How did you react? What was the outcome?

Those are the types of questions associated with this principle, and below are some from "Are Right." You can see how they are the same questions. Let's review some of the questions from the "Are Right" principle:

- Tell me about a time you disagreed with a colleague. What is the process you used to work it out?

- Tell me about a time you strongly disagreed with your manager on something you deemed to be very important to the business. What was it about and how did you handle it?

- Tell me about a time where someone openly challenged you. How did you handle this feedback?

- Give an example of when you took an unpopular stance in a meeting with peers and your leader and you were the outlier. What was it, why did you feel strongly about it, and what did you do?

- When do you decide to go along with the group decision even if you disagree? Give me an example of a time you chose to acquiesce to the group even when you disagreed. Would you make the same decision now?

We see that the "Are Right" and "Have Backbone" principles are related. Show your interviewer that you have the courage to fight for your ideas.

How to answer the questions related to "Have Backbone"
Having to fight for your idea may make you uncomfortable. It makes me uncomfortable because I don't like competitiveness or aggression (especially directed at me!). If this type of culture intimidates you, give extra attention to your preparation for interview questions related to conflict. If you're unable to answer the questions directly, you may come across as someone who lacks the backbone to work in a competitive environment. And Amazon really does have a culture of "sharp elbows" so if you want the job, you'll need to hide your discomfort with conflict or at least show it won't stand in the way of your leadership. On the other hand, if you're someone who thrives in competitive environments, be prepared to demonstrate that you can manage conflict calmly and rationally, that you can convince others with data, not by yelling or being unnecessarily aggressive.

If you're in an Amazon interview and you're asked how you've dealt with workplace conflict in the past, consider the following approach:

1. First, summarize for the interviewer an idea that you had. Tell a story about how you were convinced that your idea was the right way forward.

2. Next, discuss the point of contention. After you explain your idea, describe how and why someone didn't agree with your idea. Then, discuss what tactic you used to win the other person over. A good way to impress your interviewer is to describe how you used data in making your argument.

3. Finally, if you were unsuccessful in persuading others, explain that you "committed" regardless. It's okay if you lost the argument, but demonstrate that you were mature enough to support the decision that the company chose. On the other hand, if you were successful in winning support for your idea, skip this step.

In these "Backbone" stories, focus on the disagreement between you and another person (or persons). Your goal should be to demonstrate how you managed the conflict itself, so don't fast forward over it. What did you say? What did the other person say? Did you have a meeting? Did you look at data together? I've found that my clients sometimes want to say very little about the actual disagreement and are eager to rush to the solution, which is a mistake. Dwell more on the details of the conflict. I know it may be boring to relate the actual conversations you had, and normally I think that's too much detail for these stories, but talking about the details is the only way to show how you handle the interpersonal aspect of conflict.

And you can add some drama. I won't usually advise you to make your stories "dramatic" because this is an interview, not entertainment, but these "Backbone" stories can be inherently dramatic because of the conflict factor, and that's okay.

Question: Describe a situation where others you were working with on a project disagreed with your ideas. What did you do?

Answer given by an **Engineering Manager**:

"When I was leading the Engineering team at Bank of America in India, I proposed to my U.S. partner that we build architecture capabilities in India. I thought that this would save us money. He was not convinced because he felt that the Architecture team needed to collocate with users for a better understanding of user needs, and so needed to be in the U.S.

I still believed that my idea would work, so I proposed that, instead of hiring an Architect, we test my idea and assign a Senior Developer in India to work with the U.S. Architecture team. My U.S. partner was amenable to this approach as a "pilot project."

I onboarded a Senior Developer, and he started working with the Architecture team remotely. He was working on a migration project from Oracle to SAP. This Developer, now functioning as a remote member of the Architecture team, was able to offer significant contributions to the project from India. He created a proof of concept for moving data across systems, which the team ultimately used as a framework for other work. He also helped the onshore team prepare architecture diagrams.

Once the offshore Architect started delivering from India, my U.S. partner's perspective on the matter began to shift. He asked me to ramp up the Architecture team with more remote team members. After building this team, overall delivery improved as offshore had become an extended capability to complement the existing onshore team."

This story shows that the Engineering Manager was willing to take different approaches to get her idea across, which is great. However, the story would be stronger if it included more details about how she dealt with the conflict with her U.S. partner. When you are telling a story about how you "Have Backbone," don't shy away from talking about the confrontation itself, and how you behaved in that situation. Don't just rush to the outcome.

Question: Was there a time when you were right but your senior colleagues didn't agree with you?

Answer given by a **UX Designer**:

"The project was helping the Marketing team create campaigns. I had designed a low-fidelity wireframe option and was reviewing it with Product Management and Engineering. Our user was supposed to click on the "Create New Campaign" button, which would then take them to "Create Mode." After applying a set of filters, the user would then click "Save," and the campaign page would then go into the "Read Only" mode. At that point, the filters are not accessible to the user. To access the filters again, the user had to click the "Edit Campaign" button. Product Management and Engineering did not like this flow because they thought that the user should always be in "Edit" mode.

I tried to convince them that my flow was a common design pattern that users would find familiar, demonstrating for example how users added contacts on their phones. They showed me an old desktop enterprise product and said that it was better. Since I was struggling to convince them, I created a flow that was in line with their suggestion and requested that they participate in a usability test of that flow. To me, this usability test was not strictly necessary because I knew from experience that users would find my proposed solution more intuitive and easier to use. I went ahead regardless to convince my colleagues.

I had a group of users try "Option A" (which was my flow) and another group of users try "Option B" (which was their flow). I performed the usability tests with my colleagues so that they could see for themselves how users interacted with each flow. The test results showed what users preferred and how they interact with interfaces of this type. We went with Option A."

This story is interesting because the UX Designer sticks to his principles in the face of adversity. Both Product and Engineering are aligned against him, and it would have been easier for him to just agree with them. But as a UX Designer, he must put users first. That's his role on the team. So he patiently set up the test to guide his colleagues toward a better way.

Deliver Results
The fourteenth Amazon Leadership Principle is "Deliver Results." If you're preparing for an interview at Amazon, you should ask yourself what the company means by delivering results and how this principle relates to the role you're applying for.

Let's look at how Amazon explains the "Deliver Results" principle:

Leaders focus on the key inputs for their business and deliver them with the right quality and in a timely fashion. Despite setbacks, they rise to the occasion and never settle.

What does the "Deliver Results" principle mean?

In many ways, this is the most important principle.

Delivering results is the one thing you absolutely must do if you work at Amazon. The other principles are important, but they're merely building blocks to this one. In the words of the principle itself, if you "rise to the occasion" – meaning succeed in what you were doing – you've shown yourself to be a leader.

You may be asking yourself, "What is the point of the other principles if you don't actually have to follow them?" I can understand your confusion because you've been studying the other principles, and now I'm telling you that they're not crucial. It's not that the other principles aren't important, because they are. It's just that you need to think of them as the building blocks, and look at "Deliver Results" as the final product. The others are intended to be the steps you need to take to get results.

How to answer questions related to "Deliver Results"

So how do you show in your answers that you've delivered results? You need to tell stories about successes.

You can use a phrase like this to show your investment in delivering results:

"I was able to have a lot of responsibility and decision-making ability for X project, and by doing Y tasks, I delivered results in Z number of launches."

In this phrase, you talk about the tasks you did to create a particular result. This will fit easily into your PAR format answer – the situation or problem is the project you were working on and the action step is the tasks you did in order to create successful results.

Interview questions related to "Deliver Results"
If your interviewer asks about this leadership principle, she or he might ask one of the following questions:

- Describe a situation where you had to face a particularly challenging situation while working on a project and what you did to overcome it. (Note: The challenge could be with respect to timeline, scope, people, or a combination thereof.)

- How you check your progress against your goals?

- Do you set and communicate smart team goals, expectations, and priorities? Do you help employees stay focused/help remove barriers/roadblocks towards meeting team goals?

- Tell me about a time you were able to persevere through setbacks and overcome obstacles to deliver outstanding results.

- Tell me about a time you not only met the goal but considerably exceeded expectations. How were you able to do it?

- What's the most complex problem you've ever worked on?

- Have you ever worked on something really hard and then failed?

Sample answers for "Deliver Results"
Question: Tell me about a time you not only met your goals, but exceeded expectations.

212

Answer given by a **Senior Technical Account Manager**:

"There was one time when I was working as a consultant for USAF. On one of the daily standup calls, the client (USAF Project Manager) mentioned that most of his other applications do smart card authentication. He wanted to add that feature to the Oracle Application I was working on.

So, even though this wasn't a formal request from him I ran with it. I started a conversation with Oracle on understanding the products we could leverage to get job done. I set up meetings with their Product teams, got to know the product, discussed our requirements, and decided that we could come up with a solution. I implemented that solution in our development environment. I had the proof of concept done before the next sprint started in four weeks.

I just about knocked the Project Manager's socks off when I showed him that POC! The feature wasn't technically part of the project plan, and he had no idea I would try to add it. He was really pleased."

I like this story because the Account Manager says a lot about himself in a succinct and relatable way. He answers the question exactly and shows he goes above and beyond when he "Drives Results." It comes natural to him, and he takes pride in it. (And yes, he got the job!)

Question: Describe a situation where you had to face a particularly challenging situation while working on a project and what you did to overcome it.

Answer given by an **Agile Coach**:

"Our company recently migrated from SDLC to Agile. It was a difficult transition due to the mindset of my peers. They were used to delivering projects in a waterfall methodology for such a long time it was difficult for them to completely accept Agile principles.

I had already delivered a large project with Agile using Jira as the tool while working very closely with our business partners and analysts. I could see my manager was struggling with bringing everyone completely on board. So I took the initiative of learning Rally and setting up all my peers with workspace in Rally. I also created a guide with instructions on using various functionality in Rally for them to set up their teams and how to get started with Agile ceremonies. My manager was appreciative of my efforts.

Not every organization/team was going to go Agile at the same time, so we had a large integration project this year where the team was still waterfall whereas ours was Agile. This project was an ideal candidate to form a vertical stack Agile team and collaborate throughout the year to deliver. I was able to present a case to senior management of their organization to form a cross-organizational Agile team. Today we have a cross functional and cross org Agile team that has a set cadence."

This story is about one of the most challenging parts of any business – culture change. When choosing your own stories, try to think of challenging situations that the interviewer may have experience him or herself. To "Drive Results," the Agile Coach took control of the situation by learning new tools and methodologies, and then introduced those concepts to his immediate team. He then used what he learned to drive change in other parts of the organization.

Strive to be Earth's Best Employer

The fifteenth Amazon leadership principle is "Strive to be the Earth's Best Employer." If you're preparing for an interview at Amazon that involves managing people, you should practice answering questions based on this leadership principle.

This is how Amazon explains the principle:

Leaders work every day to create a safer, more productive, higher performing, more diverse, and more just work environment. They lead with empathy, have fun at work, and make it easy for others to have fun. Leaders ask themselves: Are my fellow employees growing? Are they empowered? Are they ready for what's next? Leaders have a vision for and commitment to their employees' personal success, whether that be at Amazon or elsewhere.

What does the "Earth's Best Employer" leadership principle mean?

This new principle is related to <u>leadership principle #6, Hire and Develop the Best</u>, but takes the ideas in #6 a few steps further. "Hire and Develop the Best" says that a leader will "recognize exceptional talent, and willingly move them throughout the organization. Leaders develop leaders and take seriously their role in coaching others." "Hire and Develop" says that a leader should care about an employee's success and be working with high performers to grow their careers. Now the new principle expands the duties of a leader.

There are a lot of new ideas packed into the principle, so I'm going to group some together to make it easier to process.

Safety

The new principle introduces the idea of safety / a safe work environment. This is a concept most relevant to the Level 1-3 employees, like warehouse workers, drivers, and so on. These are the workers that complained during the pandemic that the company didn't care about their health, and they are the workers most at risk for accidents at work. A leader is now supposed to give more serious thought to their workers' safety.

Diversity

The principle also introduces the word "diverse." Many people had been calling for Amazon to hire more diverse employees, since most of the top leaders are white men. Instead of creating a new principle for diversity, they've added the diversity idea into this principle. A leader should strive to create a more diverse team. That was already one idea under the "Hire" principle, but now it's explicitly listed.

Just

The principle also introduces the word "just," which the dictionary defines as "based on or behaving according to what is morally right and fair." Morality, the difference between right and wrong, is now important for leaders at Amazon.

Fun

Having fun at work yourself and creating fun for your employees is now a leader's task.

Empathy is taking into consideration what employees are feeling and going through. Leading with empathy means taking the time to understand their point of view. If you think about it, in some ways, this is like principle #1, which is "Customer Obsession" and has historically been the most foundational principle. "Obsessing" over customers means working to understand their problems and finding ways to overcome those problems. In other words, to show true "Customer Obsession," leaders must have empathy for the customer. Now, with the introduction of this fifteenth principle, Amazon is asking its leaders to apply that same empathy for employees.

More productive / higher performing / focused on employee's personal success, growth, and empowerment
These are fairly standard ideas for managing a team; they would make just as much sense under "Hire and Develop."

Interview questions related to "Earth's Best Employer"
If your interviewer asks about this leadership principle, he or she might ask one of the following questions:

- What routines have you established in your workplace to improve safety?

- Describe a time you constructed a team. What factors did you consider? Did you factor in diversity? How did you balance work requirements, team skill composition, and team stretch opportunities? How did you allocate work? How did you ensure team members were able to work effectively together?

- What is the composition of your current team, and how is your team organized?

- How do you deal with managing at team of different backgrounds, levels, and skills?

- How do you tell the difference between "right" and "wrong" as it applies to your job? What does it mean to you to be a "just" manager?

- How have you made your employees excited about coming to work?

- Tell me about a time when you made the wrong assumptions about a direct report or a peer. How did you unearth the wrong assumption? How did you correct it? How did you prevent it from happening again?

- Tell me how you help your team members develop their careers. Can you give me two to three examples of a specific person in whom you invested and how you helped them develop their careers, including one who wasn't being successful but in whom you saw potential and chose to invest?

- Give me an example of a time you provided feedback to develop and leverage the strengths of someone on your team. Were you able to positively impact that person's performance? What were your most effective methods?

- How do you manage your top performers differently?

- Give me an example of someone who was promoted one or two levels up in the organization, not just because they were a star who would naturally rise, but due to your coaching efforts.

- How have you been successful at empowering either a person or a group to accomplish a task.

- Tell me about a time when you were able to remove a serious roadblock preventing your team from making progress.

How many stories do I need for this principle?
Most people say that you should have two examples for each principle. That's a good benchmark but doesn't really work for this one. You need to have stories to answer questions in all of the categories under this principle — safety, diversity, productivity, managing low and high performers, and so on. If you're going for a manager job, you need to show all of the skills a manager needs, not just one. And these categories tend to be unique — a story about improving workplace safety isn't going to work for a question about having fun at work, for example.

How to answer interview questions about the "Earth's Best Employer" Amazon leadership principle
The key to answering these questions is to demonstrate certain skills in your answers. You'll want to show that:

- **You care about safety.**

    Safety is a broad category that can be very different depending on which industry or job function you work in. Ask yourself what employee "safety" means in your line or work and/or for the job you're applying to.

    If you're an Area Manager at a warehouse, you should be able to talk about the safety processes you have implemented and how you measure them. This example is relatively straightforward since you can speak to how you prioritized the physical safety of your peers or your reports.

What about less straightforward examples? Keep in mind that "safety" can take on other meanings, for example, "emotional safety" or "psychological safety." If you're a Development Manager, for example, the physical safety of your employees is relatively less important than it would be for, say, an Area Manager. But emotional and psychological safety are just as important. How did you create and contribute to a work environment that is emotionally safe? How did you make it clear to your reports and your peers that they can express their professional opinions, even ones that you dislike, without fear of repercussions? How did you, as a Development Manager, respond to what you perceived as poorly written code? Or when an employee failed to meet clear expectations?

Those are just a couple of examples to help you brainstorm. As you prepare for your interview, just remember that there are many types of "safety," and you should think about which is most important to your line of work.

- **You value people who are not like you.**

Tech has a diversity problem.

If you're a white man (which many of my clients are), you may not be very aware of the diversity issue. If you've created a team that isn't all white men, consider it an accomplishment and be prepared to speak to it. How did you make diversity a priority?

If you're an Indian man working in tech, you may not be used to working on a team with many women. If you've created a team that has women on it, be sure to include them in your answers. Make sure you don't refer to your team as "guys." When you talk about your users or your clients, do you always refer to them as "he"? I have so many clients who tell story after story and there are no women in any of them. If you're a team leader, this reflects badly on you.

A diverse team will give you teammates who can understand your customer better than you can. It will also provide more, different skills for you to draw from in creating better products for your customers. A savvy manager understands that having multiple viewpoints on a team makes the team better able to help more customers. Ultimately, if you can understand the customer you can probably sell to them, but if you can't relate to the customer (because you don't have anyone on your team with the right viewpoint or skills) you can't sell to them.

- **You recognize strong performers and mentor them.**

If you currently work at a company where the attention goes to low performers, you should reorient yourself. Amazon believes that spending time on top performers is one of the best uses of a leader's time, so don't say that you spend an equal amount of time mentoring low performers. Low performers should be coached to improve their performance quickly or managed out quickly. Avoid stories where you coach an employee for six months or a year before their performance improves.

You try to help your people grow. You make it a priority to coach and teach employees. You provide regular feedback.

Show that you know what each employee wants and that you are trying to help them achieve that goal. You help employees drive their own development and learning by regularly discussing career goals, strengths, and areas for development. Show that you identify development activities and career moves for all employees.

Sample answers for the "Earth's Best Employer" principle

Question: Talk to me about how you've prioritized hiring a diverse set of team members.

Answer by a **Director of Engineering**:

"When I was hired as Director of Engineering at my current company, I was concerned by the lack of diversity on the staff. My predecessor hired Software Developers two years out of specific university programs that he believed were the best. What we had as a result was a team of smart people in their early to mid 20s with very similar backgrounds and ethnicity who had only learned about enterprise scale architecture in an academic setting or had limited exposure via internships. But based on where the organization was headed, I needed people who had already built enterprise scale architecture, shipped it, maintained and upgraded it over years, and replaced it when needed. Also, I knew that a more diverse team brings a wider spectrum of

approaches for solving problems, which in turn yields higher productivity and more robust systems, as long as you build a culture where different points of view are valued.

My first step was to categorize my 50+ team members in terms of age, race, experience, sex, educational background, and several other data points. I enlisted my HR team for help, and it turned out that they had helped other managers in the company with similar efforts. I learned my team was 83% male, 92% white, 87% had come from the same four schools, and no one was over the age of 27. Only 10% of them had worked in an enterprise software setting for more than two years.

Based on this data, I worked with HR on a new recruiting program. We discarded the university background requirement, opening up the possibility of candidates with less traditional backgrounds (e.g., not in Computer Science). Experience was given the same importance as education. We also set targets related to demographics. For example, we set a target of increasing the number of female hires. In setting these targets, we compared ourselves to our peers in the same industry and sought to exceed industry standards.

After a three-year effort I managed to hit my initial targets. I built the most diverse team in the company. In terms of impact, because we had a rich set of experience and backgrounds, we created something entirely new, an open source framework for managing distributed data at scale. I'm convinced this wouldn't have been possible had we stayed on our previous trajectory. Our number of male employees dropped from 83% to 73% within one year. Also, a huge bonus was an increase in retention. The average *amount of time a developer stayed at the company increased by 32%. The HR team started applying my team-building approaches more broadly."*

Just because the leadership principles changed in 2021, the structure for answering behavioral questions about the principles is the same. When creating your own stories about these new principles, remember to use the PAR structure, just as the Director of Engineering does in the answer above.

Question: Tell me how you motivate your team to meet key performance indicators while still having fun and keeping morale high.

Answer given by a **Plant Manager**:

"In my current role, I manage a print on demand plant, which consists of ten printers running simultaneously, with a crew assigned to each printer. The team is experienced and has hit its numbers pretty regularly, until recently. Starting last year, we started receiving order sizes that were on average much smaller than what we had seen in the past. Smaller orders take longer, and so we started missing our numbers. Something had to be done.

After a few weeks of this, I started to think maybe we needed to change the KPIs for the new normal. Instead, I decided to have an "idea" competition, where each crew would propose an idea for working differently for one week. We'd try it, and if we saw an improvement, we'd double down on the idea. This competition wasn't a tough sell. The crews love to compete and many of them had ideas to improve production rates. Tired of the doom and gloom from not meeting our numbers, I decided to make things fun. I decided that each team should name itself after the superhero that best represented their idea. For example, the team who experimented with new technology called itself The Batman because he always used high-tech gadgets. Everyone got into it, and we even went so far as to create a competition bracket, which was pretty funny with the different team names. On this bracket, you'd see, like, Wonder Women versus Groot and all sorts of hilarious stuff like that.

But it wasn't just a joke. I was deadly serious about getting us back to hitting our numbers under these new conditions. The best idea came from a crew called the X-Humans, which introduced the idea of flexible crew sizes based on order size. They called these new teams "Mutant Crews." This meant that, on any given day, crew makeup and size would shift according to need. It sounds simple, but truthfully, it never even occurred to me. I thought crews were tight and needed to operate as units. Turned out, we needed something totally new, and these Mutant Crews adapted quickly. We started hitting our KPIs again, and I even started to think they were too low. Senior management loved hearing that."

Elements of this story are silly, but it takes confidence to show you're not afraid to be silly if it means hitting a KPI, while simultaneously having fun. This story really captures the spirit of the fifteenth principle.

Success and Scale Bring Broad Responsibility

The sixteenth Amazon Leadership Principle is "Success and Scale Bring Broad Responsibility." This is how Amazon explains the principle:

We started in a garage, but we're not there anymore. We are big, we impact the world, and we are far from perfect. We must be humble and thoughtful about even the secondary effects of our actions. Our local communities, planet, and future generations need us to be better every day. We must begin each day with a determination to make better, do better, and be better for our customers, our employees, our partners, and the world at large. And we must end every day knowing we can do even more tomorrow. Leaders create more than they consume and always leave things better than how they found them.

What does the "Success and Scale " leadership principle mean?

The "Success and Scale" principle is Amazon recognizing its immense impact, on its customers, its employees, its partners, and the larger community. It challenges leaders at Amazon to acknowledge and account for this impact as a normal part of doing business.

This is the key sentence in the principle: We must begin each day with a determination to make better, do better, and be better for our customers, our employees, our partners, and the world at large.

If we break down that sentence, we'll start to see some familiar patterns that are consistent with other principles. For example, "be better for our customers" sounds a lot like leadership principle #1, "Customer Obsession."

The next part of that key sentence from principle #16 is "be better for our employees," which may remind you of leadership principle #6, "Hire and Develop the Best" and principle #15, "Strive to be Earth's Best Employer." If you're not familiar with how to show you care about your employees, read about these other two principles.

After customers and employees the principle mentions "Be better for our partners." The idea behind this phrase is similar to caring about customers, but extends this mindset to partners. If you do deal with partners, think about the stories you've created for "Customer Obsession" about helping customers. You could possibly reframe those stories so that they show how you've helped or prioritized your partners. If you're in a job that includes working with partners, you may have been thinking of them as your customers and created these stories already. If you don't deal with partners, you won't be asked about those relationships.

"Be better for the world at large." This phrase and way of working hasn't really been covered by the previous leadership principles. This addition seems like a response to the media, societal, and government scrutiny that Amazon has been getting over the past few years. What does this addition to the principles mean for you and your candidacy at Amazon?

When you are preparing to answer questions for this principle, my advice is to focus on the impact your work has had beyond your company and your customers. Depending on the types of companies you've worked for or your roles in those companies, you may need to brainstorm a bit to come up with good stories for your interview. In all likelihood, you can draw a direct line between your activities in your previous jobs and the benefit those activities had on the company and the customers. Now try to think beyond that.

For example, what about the communities in which those customers live? Did your work affect those communities? How did that factor into your thinking and planning?

Interview questions related to "Success and Scale"
If your interviewer asks about this leadership principle, he or she might ask one of the following questions:

About customers: See the questions under "Customer Obsession."

About employees: See the questions under "Hire and Develop the Best" and "Strive to be the Earth's Best Employer."

About partners:

- Tell me about a time you had to evaluate a potential strategic partnership. What approach did you take? Did you perform your evaluation using any particular framework?

- How have you developed and maintained a partner relationship?

- When did you have a difficult situation with a partner? What was the problem and how did you resolve it?

- When did you have to say no to a partner? How did you handle it?

- Have you ever lost a partner? What was the situation?

- When have you gone out of your way to help a partner?

- When have you done something to improve the process for your partner?
- Tell me about a time you worked with a partner to achieve scale that would have otherwise been impossible.

About the world:

- As you conduct internal and external business activities, how do you promote and maintain social, ethical, and organizational norms?
- Tell me about how you think about your work impacting the world.
- Tell me about a time you failed to anticipate the secondary effects of a project you worked on. How did you prevent this from happening in future projects?

How many stories do I need for this principle?

Most people say that you should have two examples for each principle. That's a good benchmark for this one, although you can see under "Hire and Develop" there are many subcategories, so if you are a people manager two isn't going to be enough.

How to answer interview questions about the "Success and Scale" Amazon leadership principle
The key to answering these questions is to demonstrate certain skills in your answers. You'll want to show that:

- You understand what it means to work at a large scale, meaning products and initiatives that could impact millions of people.

- You have enough humility to know that, even when you've had successes, you recognize the opportunities for further improvements.

- You don't "settle" for success and have a mindset that seeks to improve and optimize.

- You think deeply about the impact your work has on customers, partners, and communities, and you seek to account for secondary and potentially unintended consequences of that work.

Sample answers for the "Success and Scale" principle

Question: Tell me about a time you worked with a partner to achieve scale that would have otherwise been impossible.

Answer by a **Business Development Manager**:

"I worked in BizDev for X, a SaaS company, focused primarily on market opportunities for expansion. Our product had broad appeal across a number of markets and customer segments. The problem was that some of the most attractive markets were difficult to penetrate, and our standard way of selling into those markets wouldn't work. I was specifically interested in the government sector, which is highly regulated as you can imagine. We lacked the relationships, the regulatory compliance, and the experience to sell into government agencies, but as I said, our product was highly desirable to the customers there. My solution was to partner with resellers.

Before I was brought on, the company had considered using resellers, but the exec team, and the CFO in particular, thought the cost was too high. If you're unfamiliar with just how difficult it is to enter the government sector, then yes, the cost, usually 25% or so, does seem high, so I definitely understood the hesitation. But in many ways, using a reseller in this situation was a no-brainer. I just had to help the rest of the organization see that. Working with a financial analyst on the CFO's team, I modeled the time and cost associated with using a reseller versus trying to sell into the government space alone. The time and cost to achieve regulatory compliance alone justified using a reseller, but I did the work regardless. I used the results of the financial model to write up a proper business case, and I presented that case to the exec team.

To my surprise, they were still hesitant and felt like they needed to run it by the board. Fortunately, the board included members who had seen deals like the one I was proposing bear fruit, and we received approval to work with resellers. From there, it was just a matter of finding the right reseller for us. Within one year from the time I submitted my proposal, we had made our first sale to a government agency through our reseller. That deal was small, just five figures, but as I had hoped, it opened the door for us and over the course of the next two years, the government became a multimillion dollar revenue stream for the organization. I went on to use the same reseller framework to expand into other markets, such as the higher ed academic space."

Question: Tell me about a time you failed to anticipate the secondary effects of a project you worked on. How did you prevent this from happening in future projects?

Answer given by a **VP of Maintenance and Operations**

"I was working for a company that built and leased cell towers to the big cell phone providers. We were responsible for the maintenance and operation of the towers, and I headed up the maintenance team for all North American towers. You might be surprised to hear this, but our biggest cost was the on-site inspections, which were required as a part of the leasing terms. Honestly, I thought monthly inspections were unnecessary, but I had to abide by the terms, and so every month for every tower, we sent someone on site for a full inspection. I should add that these inspections were dangerous. While we had had just a few injuries (and no fatalities), the thought of an equipment failure that led to someone on my team falling from the top of one of those towers kept me up at night.

Our company had a goal to go public within two years, and ahead of that, I was eager to reduce costs and increase safety without cutting corners on the inspections. After some research and analysis with the team, we determined that we could begin using drones to meet the terms of the license, and we were comfortable that we could check everything else from the ground. Twice a year, we'd still have to send someone up the tower for a closer inspection, but for the rest, the drones would cover it. This approach would cut the time for an inspection by a third, and of course, much safer all around. Win-win, right? I couldn't wait to present this plan to the higher-ups.

To my surprise, not everyone shared my excitement, which in all honesty was a huge miss on my part. While the union was happy about the increase in safety, they objected to the potentially reduced work hours and also the inspectors lacked the expertise to operate the drones. Many team members were very concerned about losing their jobs all together. In my excitement, I had failed to consider the impact on them, their jobs, and their families. In the end, we were able to address this by retraining the inspectors and restructuring their pay incentives, where they were actually rewarded not punished for more efficient inspections. And I learned a lesson about thinking through the implications beyond cost in creating operational efficiencies."

Chapter 14. How to Answer Correctly for Job Level

My clients will often ask me how to create answers that show their experience is the right level for the job. You can usually determine the "level" of the job you're applying for at Amazon by matching it up with the company's leveling system (ranging from L1 to L11; I cover this in more detail in Chapter 2). If you're unable to determine where the job you're applying for fits on the leveling system, you can ask the recruiter, and they'll usually be able to tell you.

Knowing where the job fits in Amazon's leveling system is helpful in determining compensation expectations for the role, but many of my clients also want to use the interview to demonstrate that they are qualified for the more senior position. For example, say you're applying for a Program Manager role – how do you show you have the right experience to be considered for Senior Program Manager instead of just Program Manager, or to come in at the middle of the Program Manager salary range, instead of at the very low end of it? How do you show you have the right experience to be hired for Principal PM instead of Senior PM?

Categories of Responsibility

To show you have the experience for the more senior level of the role or a more senior role altogether, you can use the following framework. Consider adding these pieces of information to your answers:

- Scope

- Impact

- Supervisory responsibilities

- Tactics versus strategy

- Level of ambiguity

- Process improvement

- Relationships

- Collaboration

Let's look at each of those in detail. As you read through the descriptions that follow, think about how you can weave these things into your stories. In adding this information to your stories, you're seeking to impress upon your interviewer that you have more senior experience, which will ideally end in an offer at the higher range of compensation or, even better, a more senior title (and the comp that comes with it).

Scope

The first two items on the "Categories of Responsibility" are "Scope" and "Impact," and they are closely related. For scope specifically, you want to show in your stories that the project you were working on was large. The higher the job level, the larger the project should be.

Assuming you're using the PAR method, you can include scope in the "Problem" section of your story. How you show scope of your work varies based on the role.

If you're in Sales, maybe the scope is related to the size or prestige of a client you landed. Or if you work in Product or Program Management, maybe the scope is related to the complexity of the project. Here are some ideas for you to consider including when thinking about scope:

- Size of the business (number of customers) or size of the product (number of users)
- Size of client
- Prestige of client (well-known brand)
- Yearly revenue
- Budget allocation
- The degree of risk to the company
- Project length
- Project complexity
- Number of teams involved (only yours or more?)
- Did you work in your own business unit (as you'd expect for a more junior role) or across multiple business units (more senior)?

Impact

Related to scope is "Impact" - what effect did your project have?

This is arguably the most important item on the list and fits directly into the Results section of your PAR behavioral stories. In talking about impact, be sure to include specific data points.

Because Amazon is so huge, you might want to frame impact in terms of percentages instead of raw numbers. For example, let's say you worked on a project that resulted in ten million dollars in revenue for the organization, which might sound small to someone at Amazon. Instead, say that the project resulted in a 20% increase in ARR (annual recurring revenue), which is much more impressive because it accounts for the size of the org.

While revenue and/or profit are good indicators of impact, there are many metrics you could use:

- Money coming in (revenue)
- Money you end up with (profit)
- Volume change
- Cost savings
- Percentage change, year over year improvements
- Time to market, implementation time, time savings
- Impact on the customer or the team
- Impact on business
- Quality improvements
- Customer happiness as measured by Net Promoter Score
- Retention rate
- Customer lifetime value

Whichever metrics you choose to show impact, be sure to quantify and explain volume, size, and scale.

Supervisory responsibilities

If the job includes people management, demonstrate how you effectively deployed the human resources that were available to influence how your interviewers perceive your level.

To show that you are a more senior level candidate, include in your stories:

- The size and number of teams – the larger the higher the level

- Experience supervising senior managers – the higher the level of your direct reports, the higher your own level

- Your methods for successfully motivating a team – experienced managers have given a lot of thought to motivating teams, which will come through in your answers

- Experiences in which you've delegated large projects to senior level people and gotten results

- Experiences in which you've made the most of your team members' strengths while minimizing or working around their weaknesses

Tactics versus strategy

Strategy is the long-term vision and tactics are the specific actions you use to achieve the vision.

Showing that you're able to think strategically is another way to prove to your interviewer that you have more senior-level experience. Lower-level employees are usually told to do a task and then do it, but experienced, senior-level staff will often have to decide what to do and also then plan how to do it.

To show your interviewer you're a strategic thinker, include in your stories the strategic goals of your company and how you contributed to that strategy. If you're very senior (executive level), then you likely played a key role in formulating the strategy. What was your competitive advantage and how did you make the most of it? If you weren't among the team creating the company strategy, show your interviewer that you understood it and contributed to it.

Show that you understood the why and not just the what. How did the way you managed your team fit into the big picture? How did you contribute to the long-term, multi-year plan for the company beyond the daily grind? Where did you adopt a new tactic that no one else thought of?

Even if your experience is limited to managing or working on individual projects, you should be able to include in your stories details related to how those projects fit into the larger strategic goals of your organization.

Ambiguity level

Showing your interviewer that you can navigate ambiguity is another way to prove you are a more senior candidate. An ambiguous situation happens when there is no clear path forward or, even more common, when there are many paths forward but it's unclear which path is best and why. When an ambiguous situation arises in business, a senior leader will:

- Analyze the situation
- Propose the best way forward
- Influence others to follow along

In your stories, the second two items especially are opportunities for you to convince your interviewers that you deserve to be considered a more senior-level candidate. Analysis of an ambiguous situation is, in some ways, the easy part. Deciding how to act on that analysis and convincing others that you're right is much more challenging.

Process improvements

Processes that you were responsible for or helped create provide another opportunity to distinguish yourself as a more senior candidate. We all have processes that we work within and are potentially responsible for. A more junior job candidate might talk about a process that was assigned to them or that they ran smoothly. A more senior candidate, however, should be able to tell stories far beyond keeping things running and maintaining the status quo. Candidates that want to stand out talk about processes they improved drastically. They can cite improvement metrics and the impact those improvements had on the overall business. Was there a time in your career in which you completely overhauled a process? If so, that's the story you want to tell. Even better if you can show you personally initiated these improvements because you saw something no one else saw.

The most senior-level candidates don't just improve processes. They invent entirely new processes based on an opportunity that only they themselves were able to recognize. For example, a senior-level candidate might study an emerging technology and see it could have a major impact if applied to their business processes. Or maybe the candidate has a keen eye for identifying and removing bottlenecks. Or maybe she made a series of very small improvements that, over time, accumulated into something bigger.

240

In your own stories, the key is to talk about process improvements that were transformative in how they impacted the business. Amazon is all about results, so if you want to appear more senior, map your process improvements to business impact.

Relationships

To show that you should be considered a more senior-level candidate, you must show that you have a track record of working with other senior managers. It's not enough to show you impressed an executive with a project once. For you to come across as senior, you must instead have stories that show how you built relationships with the most senior leaders at your company. The more you can show that you worked alongside these leaders as peers, the better.

Ideally, you have stories for your interview that detail how other leaders at your company came to rely on you. Maybe you were their "go-to" person in your subject area. Or maybe they wouldn't dream of making a decision in your area of expertise without first consulting you.

Relationships in business are all about trust. If you have a strong relationship with senior managers, it means they know they can count on you. Unless they're forced to or the situation is unavoidable, senior managers won't waste time with team members they don't trust. For your interview, think about experiences in which the most senior-level members of the company went out of their way to seek you out. Experiences like that will signal to your interviewer that you are reliable and can be trusted to be placed in charge of more senior-level initiatives and resources.

Collaboration

Amazon has a culture of collaboration that is very strongly based in direct, ongoing feedback. If you want to show your Amazon interviewer that you should be taken seriously as a senior candidate, you must show that you know that "collaboration" means more than just being a "team player."

Giving feedback means that you were not afraid to speak up if you saw a flaw in someone's plan, even if it might result in a confrontation. No one likes being questioned and scrutinized. But one thing that you should understand is that, the more senior you are at Amazon, the more likely that scrutiny will be the norm in your day-to-day interactions with your colleagues. Debate and discussion are a key part of collaboration, especially among senior people.

Do you have stories where you can show a healthy debate between colleagues led to a better result than was initially proposed? If so, you have the ideal story for your interviewer because you can show that you understand that collaboration isn't just going with the flow. Collaboration is about getting the best out of yourself and everyone around you, which can only come through a willingness to give direct feedback.

Putting It All Together

Let's look at the Program Manager versus Senior Program Manager through the ideas I just introduced.

Program Manager:

- Scope – Works across teams. Influences their customers, roadmap priorities, and decisions. May influence external entity interactions.

- Impact – Moderate. Multiple team goals and program-related metrics. May impact a country or region.

- Supervisory responsibilities – Mentors junior employees or peers usually unofficially.

- Tactics versus strategy – Work is tactical. Owns a small or medium sized program. Manages cross-functional projects/goals. Defines program requirements and drives team(s)/partners to meet goals. Accelerates progress by driving timely decisions. Able to spot risks, ask the right questions. Clears blockers, escalates appropriately. Makes trade-offs: time vs. quality vs. resources.

- Level of ambiguity – Program strategy is defined. Business problem and solution may not be defined. Delivers independently but will seek direction.

- Process improvements – Improves project and process efficiency. Optimizes cross-team processes that improve team efficacy and delivery.

Senior Program Manager: The responsibilities shift and are larger in scope and the work is more strategic in nature. If you look at the same categories again, note how the duties and responsibilities have changed for the more senior position:

- Scope – Works within a VP organization. Influences large customer segments, technology decisions, or external entity interaction.

- Impact – High. Sets organizational goals and program-related metrics. May have cross-region impact.

- Supervisory responsibilities – Actively mentors and develops others. Likely has other Program Managers reporting to them.

- Tactics versus strategy – Work is tactical and strategic. Owns a large program. Manages the lifecycle of complex initiatives. Unblocks teams and increases the speed of delivery. Negotiates resources and priorities. Able to find a path forward in difficult situations. Makes trade-offs between short-term needs vs. long-term needs.

- Level of ambiguity – Business problem may not be well-defined. Program strategy may not be defined. Delivers independently, with limited guidance.

- Process improvements – Improves, streamlines, and/or eliminates excess process. Drives efficiencies. Creates predictable process paths.

Chapter 15. How to Avoid Common Mistakes

Add Data to Your Answers

Amazon loves data. Your answers should have a balance of enough data but not too much. Use enough to show that you clearly can use data but if you give too many details they'll get bored. You should aim for an answer that is around three to four minutes long.

Replace adjectives with data

Whenever you can, replace adjectives with data. Here are some examples of how to do this:

Lacking data: We made the performance much faster

With data: We reduced server side tp90 latency from 10 ms to 1 ms

Lacking data: Nearly all customers

With data: 92% of Bonus-club members

Lacking data: Significantly better

With data: Up 34 points

Where does data go in your answers?

You can put the data anywhere in your answer, but the place it fits most easily (and needs to be) is in the Results section.

Types of data you can use

- Cost savings, revenue generation

- Quantify to explain volume, size, scale
- Percentage change, year over year improvements
- Time to market, implementation time, time savings
- Impact on the customer, the team
- Quality improvements

Example of an answer with data

In this scenario the candidate is the CEO of a mid-sized landscaping company. You may not be able to relate to this business, but it's a simple answer that will show you the right way to use data.

Question: You mentioned you didn't make revenue in 2019. Can you walk me through why?

Poor answer

In 2019 there wasn't as much rainfall as there had been in previous years. There was only two inches of rain. This led to a lot of our customers' grass yellowing and subsequently not being cared for by our team, which ultimately hurt revenues. We knew this might happen again so we worked on educating our customers about drought-resistant grasses and drought-resistant landscaping. This helped us in future years when there wasn't enough rain.

Better answer

Bartlett is a landscaping company that works in Texas and adjoining states. Our revenue is tied closely to rainfall because more rainfall causes plants to grow more and so our customers then need more service. In the area of Texas where we do 65% of our business the average rainfall in the summer is six inches but in 2019 it was down to two inches. This caused our revenue for that season to fall.

The grass that is most common in that area of Texas is St. Augustine, which requires at least four inches of rain to sustain a natural growth pattern. When the grass grows naturally, we are able to remain on a typical cadence of lawn service for our customers, which is bi-weekly. When the grass doesn't grow enough (like when it doesn't rain as much), customers generally cancel some of their work with us because the grass doesn't need to be cut. This is what happened in 2019.

To prevent the same loss of revenue in 2020 that we had in 2019, we needed to do as much as we could to prevent the same thing from happening again. We can't control the weather, but we hired a weather analytics firm to give us estimates of rainfall 60 days prior to summer. We also began to develop other ideas for low-rainfall year gardening, such as educating our clients about xeri-scaping (low-water requirement landscaping) and varieties of grass that require less water.

When our weather firm let us know that there might again be less rain in 2020, we rolled out these new plans with our clients. This helped us with revenue in 2020 and is also helping in 2021. It seems clear now that we will have to continue to work with lower water requirement plants given what is happening with the continuing drought in our area.

Analysis
The "Poor" answer above is very surface level and does not go into enough detail.

In the "Better answer," the candidate used data to work though the scenario.

Which of these types of data is in this answer?

- Cost savings, revenue generation
- Quantify to explain volume, size, scale
- Percentage change, year over year improvements
- Time to market, implementation time, time savings
- Impact on the customer, the team
- Quality improvements
- Revenue generation and year over year improvements

What else could be added?

Although the answer isn't bad, and does include some data, it leaves me wondering about these other points:

- The size of the business (number of customers)
- Annual revenue in year before the drought
- Revenue in years with less rain
- Number of customers who chose the drought-resistant grass
- Number of customers who switched to xeri-scaping

These are all info that can be included pretty easily without adding too much length.

Another example

Question: When did you use customer feedback to drive innovation?

When I was a program manager at X health insurance company my team was slow in fulfilling service requests for transferring protected health information. Our customers were unhappy. I had to identify areas in which our intake processes could be improved.

The stakeholders would often complain about backlogs where tickets were open for a long period with no specific turnaround time given. My team was not meeting the SLAs and requests were then escalated. We were constantly running from one emergency to another. There was no follow up on the progress of requests, which led to closure without adequate time to test the connection from end to end. This led to multiple escalations and incident ticket creation.

To fix the problems I monitored the end-to-end processes from requirement capture to technical implementation. I identified areas in which our intake processes could be improved by including additional features in the intake form to capture the right variables during project initiation. I created a standard communication procedure for business owners to inform them periodically about the status of their tickets. I implemented a five-day requirement capture timeline for the business owners. I recommended a two-day testing period after requests were fulfilled for end-to-end automation testing. I implemented SLAs and suggested that our technical teams include adequate information in the tickets on the progress of each request and send follow-up communications with our stakeholders on the timelines required to test their connections.

As a result of my efforts the team improved their process and the backlog was significantly reduced from 97% to 5%. My customers were much happier with our turnaround times.

Analysis

It's tough to answer the customer happiness questions because happiness is unquantifiable. Can you quantify the reason they were happier?

How could you add more specifics to this answer? Go through the list of possible data to add:

- Cost savings, revenue generation
- Quantify to explain volume, size, scale
- Percentage change, year over year improvements
- Time to market, implementation time, time savings
- Impact on the customer, the team
- Quality improvements

The answer already touches on:

- Impact on the customer
- Quality improvements

but both could be better with more data.

So what other data points should this job seeker add to the story? To brainstorm for ideas, try digging into why the customer was "unhappy," as stated in the opening paragraph. How do we know customers were unhappy? Were they switching to a competing product? If so, at what rate?

Beyond customer satisfaction, what were the operational impacts? Was the situation causing their department to go over budget? Was it wasting their associates' time?

The story refers to the amount of time it was taking to resolve open support tickets. That issue creates an obvious opportunity to quantify the problem: the candidate simply needs to include original time it was taking in the Situation section and how long was it taking after it was fixed in Results.

Finally, this answer would be greatly improved with some discussion of costs. Were there any costs associated with taking more time to answer tickets? Did they need more people to fix the issues, and what were the cost implications?

Read through the story again, and you may see even more opportunities to add data. Apply this same type of scrutiny to your own stories. Where are you missing opportunities to better quantify the problem and its resolution?

I vs We

Often people are trained to use "we" when talking about their work. They say "we finished the project" instead of "I finished the project."

It is definitely more polite to use "we" when talking about your work because "we" sounds like you're paying attention to your team and not trying to take all the credit for yourself. However, being polite is not the number one thing you need to do in an interview. You do want to be polite, but you need to say what you yourself did.

Your team isn't at the interview, you are. If you don't talk about your own tasks, you might get asked "But what was your role exactly in that?"

If you wrote the code, say "I wrote the code." If you wrote part of the code and a teammate wrote part of it, say "I wrote part of the code and my teammate wrote part of it." If you asked your developer to write the code and they wrote it, say "I assigned one of the members of my team to write the code." You might be tempted in these situations to say "we wrote the code" but that isn't specific enough.

When You Can't Think of an Answer

Even if you practice enough before your interview you may still get a question you don't know how to answer. What should you do if this happens?

Don't panic

Stay calm. Not knowing how to answer a question is a normal thing and it can happen to us all. If you stay calm, you'll be able to deal with it.

Emergency techniques for stalling in the interview

- **Take your time**

    You can acknowledge that the question was asked and that you're thinking about it. You can say, "That's a great question. Let me think about that."

    Then you can be silent for a few seconds before you start talking.

- **Repeat the question**

Sometimes all you need to think of an intelligent answer is a few extra seconds.

Try repeating the question.

If they ask, "Why do you want to work at Amazon?"

You can say, "Ah, you'd like to know why I want to work here. Okay."

Or you can try this, "Where do you see yourself in five years?"

"In five years, I'd like to be…"

This can buy you a few extra seconds to think of a solid response.

Ask them to repeat or rephrase the question

You can ask them to repeat or rephrase the question.

Don't use this more than once because it will look like you're not paying attention.

- **Talk about the question**

When you've tried repeating the question, try focusing on it instead. Say things like "that's a really good question" or "I was wondering when this question would come up" or "I was hoping you would address that topic."

Again, this gives you a moment to think.

I know using "fillers" isn't generally a good thing. Many people say "um" or "uh" or "you know" or other nonsense words too much. It's true, you don't really want to use fillers, and these stalling techniques are a type of filler. But it's better to stall than to say nothing.

- **Ask to answer a parallel question**

  If you know you don't have an answer, ask if you can answer a similar or parallel question.

- **Drink some water**

  Do you have a bottle of water sitting next to you? Take a drink before you answer.

- **Be honest**

  If you have no answer, you can say that, but you need to do it well.

  You can't just say "I don't have an answer for that, so let's go to the next question."

  You can admit that you can't think of an answer at the moment and ask to come back to the question later in the interview after you've had a chance to think. You can say, "I'm sorry, I can't think of an answer to that, can you ask me again at the end?"

  This isn't ideal, of course, because you're supposed to be answering their questions, but it's much better than silence. It shows you can handle an awkward situation.

  You can only use this once, so don't use it on something where you have some idea of an answer, and they may actually remember to ask you the question again at the end, so keep working on an answer as you answer the other questions.

  You also can't use this tactic on a common, easy question. If they ask, "Why did you leave your last job?" and you can't think of an answer, you have absolutely no chance of getting the job.

Think of these as emergency techniques. They can't substitute for thorough interview practice, but they can help you if things don't go as you would expect.

Chapter 16. After the Interview

If your interview's over, you're probably thinking, "Now that my interview's over, do I need to do anything else?" Yes, actually, you do need to do one more thing. What one thing is that?

Send a Thank You Note

After you finish your interview, it's important to thank the interviewer. I don't mean while you're still talking to them, although you should do this too, I mean afterward.

A quick thank you within 24 hours is expected by most interviewers.

You won't get the job only because you sent a thank you, but you'll be noticed if you don't send one.

What format should the thank you be in?

Email is the best way to send a thank you.

In some companies and industries written thank you notes are common, but in tech companies like Amazon sending a written note doesn't fit the culture. Use email.

When should you send the thank you?

Within 24 hours. If you can send it the same day, do that.

The reason you're sending the note is because you want to give the interviewer one more reason to think positively of you. If you send it after they've already made up their mind about whom to hire, what's the point? You want to send it quickly so you have a chance to influence them.

What to say in the thank you

A note that says simply "thank you for meeting with me" is nice, but what does it show? That you have manners? Manners are good, but they probably already know you have manners (I hope you showed them you have manners during your interview.)

- There are several things you can say in your note.
- You should say "thank you for meeting with me."
- You can promote yourself more by reminding them of your skills or experience.
- You can refer to something you said in your interview if you want to underline it.
- If there's something you forgot to say, say it.
- Tell them one reason you're excited to have the job.

Thank you email template

You can use this template for the basic idea and customize it or personalize it with your own ideas.

Hi [Interviewer Name],

Thank you for meeting with me today. I enjoyed learning more about the job, and I'm excited about the opportunity to join Amazon and [do whatever you would be doing].

I look forward to hearing from you about the next steps in the hiring process. Don't hesitate to contact me if I can provide additional information.

Best regards,

[Your Name]

Dear X,

I would like to take the time to thank you and the hiring team for your willingness to speak to me on Friday about the X position. I'm excited by the prospect of working for X and adding my expertise to your team.

My skills seem to be an ideal fit for the X role, and to reiterate, I feel that I could be a great asset as I am able to think and act globally in the area of X.

I enjoyed our interview and look forward to speaking with you again about the role.

Sincerely,

X

This is the same email but has one additional paragraph. I think shorter is always better in business writing, but some people don't agree and write more than I would myself. This version isn't wrong but isn't my style. If it feels right to you to add more info like this in the email then you go ahead.

Dear X,

I would like to take the time to thank you and the hiring team for your willingness to speak to me on Friday about the X position. I'm excited by the prospect of working for X and adding my expertise to your team.

My skills seem to be an ideal fit for the X role, and to reiterate, I feel that I could be a great asset as I am able to think and act globally in the area of X.

In addition to my X skills acquired during my time at X, I also bring several years of X skills to the position. Engineering is more than just design. It also needs to meet the needs of the customer.

I enjoyed our interview and look forward to speaking with you again about the role.

Sincerely,

X

Send a LinkedIn Connection Request

After you send your thank you email, you can also send a LinkedIn connection request. This is one more chance to communicate with your interviewer and make a good impression.

LinkedIn connection request template

"It was a pleasure meeting you and learning more about Amazon and the [name of position]. I'm very interested in joining your team. Please don't hesitate to reach out if you have any questions. In the meantime, I'd like to add you to my LinkedIn network."

You don't need to say any more than that with your request. And don't send them more messages over LinkedIn after the initial request unless they write to you first.

What if I don't have their email address?

If you don't know their email address, you can send the thank you in the body of the LinkedIn request instead of in an email.

About the Author

Jennifer Scupi is an interview coach and the founder of interviewgenie.com.

You won't find many interview coaches who combine corporate management experience, a graduate degree in corporate communication, and English teaching experience. Jennifer has used this combination of skills to help many people succeed at interviewing. To help candidates succeed, the recruiting team at Amazon refers clients to her.

If you need to interview to get a job at Amazon, Jennifer can help you. If you've finished the book and you want more help preparing for your interview, write to her at jennifer@interviewgenie.com.